kamera
BOOKS

www.kamerabooks.com

ALSO BY COLIN ODELL & MICHELLE LE BLANC

Anime
David Lynch
Tim Burton
Horror Films
John Carpenter
Jackie Chan
Vampire Films

Colin Odell & Michelle Le Blanc

STUDIO GHIBLI
THE FILMS OF HAYAO MIYAZAKI & ISAO TAKAHATA

FOURTH EDITION

kamera
BOOKS

This fourth edition published in 2024
First published in 2009 by Kamera Books,
an imprint of Oldcastle Books,
Harpenden, Herts, UK
www.kamerabooks.com

A CIP catalogue record for this book is available from the British Library.

ISBN
978-0-85730-584-8 (print)
978-1-84344-489-3 (epub)

2 4 6 8 10 9 7 5 3 1

Typeset in 9.5 on 14.25pt Univers Light
by Avocet Typeset, Bideford, Devon, EX39 2BP
Printed by CPI Group (UK) Ltd, Croydon, CR0 4YY

For Marika, Hiroki, Maverick and Gracie.

And for Kirsty Ann, in memoriam. With much love to Graham.

ACKNOWLEDGEMENTS

Our thanks as always to the people whose enthusiasm and support have provided invaluable assistance in the production of this book. To all the people who have entertained us in Japan – Gavin and Hanako Bell, Ono Mio and family, Akayama Kenta, Akayama Kenji, Yaegeshi Kaori and Nakaya Kazutoshi and family. Thank you to Akayama Kenta for procuring DVDs for us and sending them from Japan. Thanks to all our language teachers – Yoshiko, Taeko, Mike and Miho – who have taught us Japanese with patience, good grace and humour. And thanks to all the people with whom we've enthused at length about Ghibli and Japan: Gavin & Hanako, John, Keith & Hill, Alastair, and Gordon.

Our love to Christine and Tony and Truus, Marc and Karol, as well as Gracie and Maverick, and Marika and Hiroki.

Thanks also to Anne Hudson, Hannah Patterson, Ion Mills, Clare Quinlivan, Elsa Mathern, Claire Watts and Ellie Lavender for their support with this book.

Special thanks to Yoshiko Miura and Hanako Bell for their advice and translation expertise.

CONTENTS

9

INTRODUCTION

A teenage witch, her hair ruffled by the wind, rides her mother's broom through the open skies. A giant robot unleashes molten destruction on the soldiers who have awakened him from centuries of slumber. A city worker recalls her childhood growing up in the 1960s. The skies above Kōbe are filled with buzzing agents of death, raining down fire upon a terrified population. A burgeoning writer seeks inspiration from a quaint antiques shop. A travelling warrior becomes infatuated with a feral wolf-child in a land scarred by war. A group of young people discover love and loss during their turbulent high-school years. A girl's parents are turned into slobbering pigs. A father turns superhero, if only for a moment, when he stands up to a local biker gang. Two elated girls soar through the air inside a grinning cat bus, its headlight eyes tracing yellow streaks in the sky above the forest. Gods and monsters. Love and loss. Jubilation and despair. The horrors of war. Childhood wonder. The passion of life. Welcome to the heart-soaring, euphoric, whimsical, terrifying, compassionate and, above all else, emotional world of Studio Ghibli.

The remarkable films of Studio Ghibli show, without a shadow of a doubt, that cinema can be art. Often the terms 'art' and 'cinema' result in products that distance audiences, but Ghibli makes films that touch the soul, that can enrapture and delight everyone from toddlers to pensioners. Crucially, they retain the one thing that's frequently lacking in commercial cinema – integrity. It is this, combined with an unprecedented box-office might in their native Japan and across the world, that has allowed the animators at Studio Ghibli to continue their work without compromising their artistic vision, telling the stories they want to tell, the way they want to tell them. Animation has often been dismissed, particularly in the West, as simplistic and aimed at children but, despite their appeal to children, Ghibli's films are universal. Put simply, Studio Ghibli is the finest animation company today, a bold claim perhaps when comparing them with the mighty Pixar (huge Ghibli fans themselves), but one that is justified.

Studio Ghibli was founded in 1985 when Miyazaki Hayao brought together Takahata Isao and producer Suzuki Toshio in order to make animated films the way they wanted to make them. Years of working for various companies producing film and television programmes had left the trio eager for artistic freedom, unhindered by external studio pressures. Now, outside Hollywood, Studio Ghibli is the most profitable animation company in the world. In Japan their films top the box-office charts and run in cinemas for months on end. On the international stage they are highly regarded, having won numerous prestigious awards, including the Academy Award for Best Animated Feature for *Spirited Away* (2001), the only non-English-language film to have won in this category. Their artistry is an inspiration to filmmakers the world over. Despite making films predominantly for their home market, they are among the most critically acclaimed studios in the world.

WHAT IS AND ISN'T A STUDIO GHIBLI FILM?

Confusion often arises as to what is and is not a Studio Ghibli film. This is because Takahata and Miyazaki's styles are so distinctive and the Ghibli brand so ubiquitous that many of the films the pair worked on prior to forming the studio are often claimed as Ghibli's. This view is further clouded because an increasing number of these works are now released under the Ghibli banner, most notably Miyazaki's *Nausicaä of the Valley of the Wind* (1984), Takahata's *Gōshu the Cellist* (1982) and the pair's breezy *Panda Kopanda* films (1972 and 1973), none of which are technically Ghibli films. Further confusion has been created by the addition of the Studio Ghibli logo, a profile of their mascot Totoro, to many of the films acquired later by the studio. In this book we will be covering the major pre-Ghibli works by Takahata and Miyazaki because they are crucial to understanding the artists' development and the emergence of the Ghibli 'house style'.

BACKGROUND

There are, of course, many people working for Studio Ghibli, but the most notable are its founders. Takahata Isao was born on 29 October 1935 in Ise, the city that hosts the most sacred shrine of Japan's indigenous religion Shintō. Miyazaki Hayao was born in the modern capital Tōkyō on 5 January 1941. These were difficult and turbulent times for Japan; the long campaigns of World War Two had left the country devastated and hungry. Following Japan's defeat in 1945 the country was occupied by the United States and, although it would eventually become one of the world's leading economic powers, the early post-war years were particularly harsh.

Takahata attended the University of Tōkyō, graduating in French literature. It was French animator Paul Grimault's unfinished *Le Roi et l'oiseau* (1948, but finally finished in 1980) that intrigued him as to the possibilities of working in animation. Perhaps it was for this reason that he applied for a job as assistant director at the fledgling Tōei Dōga studio, working on features and TV shows.

Miyazaki grew up with his three brothers, father and mother, the latter a freethinking spirit who inspired her sons to question everything. As a result of his mother's long-term illness, the family had to move around the country seeking the best medical support, a situation many commentators have linked to the genesis of *My Neighbour Totoro* (1988). Miyazaki's father worked for his brother at Miyazaki Airplane, and Hayao developed a love of flying machines. He began drawing what he saw, imagining new forms of aviation. These roots would later see him designing flying machines not only for his animated movies but also specialist modeller magazines. Miyazaki expanded his drawing skills from vehicles to people when, like many growing up in the post-war years, he became inspired by manga, Japanese comics that had been popularised by artist Tezuka Osamu. Initially, Miyazaki was only an enthusiastic hobbyist, but all that changed when, following graduation in political science and economics at Gakushuin University, he too joined the growing ranks of workers at Tōei Dōga.

Although Japan had made animated films (anime) before, the tidal wave of production really took off in the early 1960s, partly because of the work of Tezuka Osamu and partly on the back of what is often acknowledged as Japan's first feature-length colour anime *Hakujaden* (*Legend of the White Serpent*, 1958). An offshoot of its parent company Tōei, one of Japan's big movie studios, Tōei Dōga quickly established itself as a major player in the burgeoning market, making feature films and, most importantly, TV anime.

Work was very labour-intensive in the factory-like studio and the workers formed a strong union. It was through these union activities that Takahata met Miyazaki, the two of them being under the wing of Ōtsuka Yasuo, their mentor at the studio. It was Ōtsuka who recommended that Takahata be promoted to director on *Horusu: Prince of the Sun* (1968), his first feature. Takahata brought in Miyazaki as designer. Unfortunately, the film was a financial flop and Takahata eventually left Tōei along with some of the staff who had worked on *Horusu*, including Miyazaki. The pair continued to have a strong working relationship over the years although their paths would often diverge. Their first real breakthrough came with *Panda Kopanda*, which Takahata directed and for which Miyazaki provided the story, design and key animation. The mid-1970s were a particularly busy time for the pair as they fine-tuned their skills, notably on a series of immensely popular adaptations of classic literature for Nippon Animation. Miyazaki took the director's chair, and a few more besides, in the ambitious science-fiction fantasy *Conan, the Boy in Future* (1978), working once more with Ōtsuka Yasuo, as well as Takahata.

As the pair's reputations grew, opportunities arose to branch out into feature-film production. Takahata returned with *Downtown Story* (aka *Chie the Brat*, 1981) and the charming fable *Gōshu the Cellist* (1982). Miyazaki, meanwhile, had been given his first chance at feature directing on the action comedy *Lupin III: Castle of Cagliostro* (1979), but, despite the film's critical success, it didn't lead to any further film work so he returned to television animation. A slowdown in his animation workload led to Miyazaki drawing an *ad hoc* manga, *Nausicaä of the Valley of the Wind*. Partway into the series, Miyazaki had to suspend creating the manga because its success had led the magazine's production company to green-light a modestly budgeted anime of the as-yet-unfinished saga. Miyazaki brought in Takahata to produce the film. Other people involved in the project, including composer Joe Hisaishi and Suzuki Toshio, would become crucial to the look, feel and running of Studio Ghibli. *Nausicaä of the Valley of the Wind* was an unqualified commercial and artistic success. The company that had bankrolled the film agreed to help fund a new venture, an animation studio where the artists and directors called the shots, where freedom of expression would be the driving force over commercial considerations. All the work would be produced in Japan and the studio's employees would be treated as artists. Together with Takahata and Suzuki, Miyazaki formed Studio Ghibli.

With hindsight it is easy to see how Studio Ghibli became so successful, but the ride was not easy. Producing a quality animated film is very costly and has a long gestation time. A single failure at the box office would have signalled the end of the company and it was to be a number of years before Ghibli would enjoy financial security. Although regarded as classics now, the early films of Studio Ghibli did not match the box-office dynamite of *Nausicaä of the Valley of the Wind*. *Laputa: Castle in the Sky* (1986) and the double bill of *Grave of the Fireflies* (1988) and *My Neighbour Totoro* did reasonably well at the box office but were not stellar hits and the studio only started to show a respectable return on its product after the release of *Kiki's Delivery Service* (1989). After that, a series of hugely successful films followed which, coupled with the revenue generated by merchandise sales following the belated accolades given to *My Neighbour Totoro*, enabled the studio to become buoyant enough to take financial knocks with experiments like the TV movie *Ocean Waves* (1993) and Takahata's ambitious, all-digital *My Neighbours the Yamadas* (1999).

Ghibli had become a national treasure, its films frequently topping Japan's box-office charts, its popularity also soaring in Western countries following an Oscar win for Miyazaki's *Spirited Away*. One of the studio's strengths is the diversity of its output. Western perceptions of animation are generally that the format is most suited to the child or family markets, and the most popular Ghibli films remain the fantasy animations, but anime is a remarkably diverse art form. An interesting aspect, which can sometimes appear strange to Western viewers, is that many of these stories are set in the real world. This is a common feature of anime but less so in Western cinema where these types of stories would often be produced as live-action films. The studio has made both original stories and adaptations in a wide range of genres – fantasies, adventures, biopics or dramas – with narratives that can be very simple or incredibly sophisticated. As Ghibli has become more renowned, its films have become more intricate and demanding and it is the quality of the productions – the studio's commitment to artistry – that will ensure that its works remain timeless, even though animation techniques have altered dramatically in the years since Ghibli's inception.

*We purposely don't make sequels of films that become hits...
for better or for worse, we don't take the easy route... We
create films by working as hard as we possibly can and by
pushing conditions to their limit. What we wanted to do was
to create animation that has some meaning and was worth
making.* (Miyazaki, *Animage*, Tokuma Shoten, May 1991,
reprinted *Starting Point*, 2009)

Each director develops stories around themes that interest them personally but the strength of their films lies in their clear ability to tell a story and tell it well. Although it was established with an aim of developing new talent, the studio's output has been dominated by the films of its founders.

Miyazaki remains Studio Ghibli's most renowned director and it is easy to see why. His films are wonderfully inventive, soaring flights of imagination that invoke a sense of wonder in the viewer. Working predominantly in the fantasy genre (with the exception of *The Wind Rises* [2013], itself heavily fictionalised),

Miyazaki has explained that the joy of animation came from his ability to create worlds: 'If I were asked to give my view, in a nutshell, of what animation is, I would say it is "whatever I want to create"', (Miyazaki, *Animation: Monthly Picture Book Special*, March 1979, reprinted *Starting Point*, 2009).

Miyazaki's films are beautifully crafted and his style highly distinctive. He has a very hands-on approach to the creative process and prefers traditional animation techniques, storyboarding his tales using pencil and paper. He doesn't use a script; the narrative develops with the storyboards and he often doesn't know how the plot will evolve. He understands how important it is that the worlds he creates are realistic (even in a fantasy context), and that the audience must believe them. Miyazaki often encourages his viewers to think like children, regardless of the age of his protagonists: to explore and question the world he presents. Adults may have to cast logic aside and accept his alternative, but clearly defined, vision. Miyazaki often fools us by establishing his films ostensibly in the real world and then demanding that we reject our notions of physics, biology and geography, albeit in a manner that is consistent with the world he is drawing us into, even if it appears to be familiar to us. He stated in an interview with *Midnight Eye* in 2002 that, 'I try to dig deep into the well of my subconscious. At a certain moment in that process, the lid is opened and very different ideas and visions are liberated.' Miyazaki's films possess an honesty that makes even the most happy of endings credible because they do not detract from the precedents set in the narrative. Western fantasy cinema frequently demands both narrative and story closure – a resolution to the plot as well as confirmation that the future will be bright for the heroes. While most of Miyazaki's films result in an optimistic conclusion, they don't always offer an easy way out, for events of the past cannot be undone and the protagonists must strive to succeed in their future lives. Miyazaki creates well-rounded characters, who cannot simply be depicted as 'good' or 'bad'; his 'villains' are not clearly defined as such, they are depicted as complex characters with believable motivations, if indeed they are present at all. *My Neighbour Totoro*, for example, features no characters with negative traits. Additionally, many of his lead protagonists are independent and highly capable girls or young women.

As co-founder of Studio Ghibli and Miyazaki's colleague and close friend since their early days at Tōei, the importance of Takahata Isao's influence on both Miyazaki and the studio cannot be underestimated. Known to his friends as Paku-san, his working method was completely opposite to Miyazaki's; he was, in his friend's own words, 'the descendant of a giant sloth'. He was a perfectionist, taking his time to produce the highest quality and most detailed work he could. Miyazaki went on to note that 'Suzuki san... and others realized they had to somehow corral the sloths and drive them towards the finish line ' (Miyazaki 1990, reprinted in *Starting Point*, 2009)

When Suzuki Toshio engaged Nishimura Yoshiaki to produce *The Tale of Princess Kaguya* (2013), he knew that 'in order to bring Takahata-san's film to fruition, I needed someone who could stick with him 24 hours a day'. As a director Takahata was naturally closely involved with the creative process but had a more hands-off approach to the actual animation, preferring to use the creative talents of others. 'If you want to make an animated film from your own drawings, I think you would become very narrow and limited by your own style and abilities. The role of the director is to gather very talented people, and to direct his vision.' (*LA Times*, 21 October, 2014)

Takahata often, but not exclusively, chose to adapt literary works – whether from novels, manga or even comic strips – and many of these films are set in the real world. Additionally, his films are generally set in Japan and many reference Japanese culture, particularly its folk tales, poetry, mythical creatures and history.

Whereas Miyazaki's drawing and animation style is distinctive and largely consistent across his entire output, Takahata was more willing to experiment with different approaches to animation and storytelling techniques. The visual style of *Grave of the Fireflies* is so different to *My Neighbours the Yamadas* or *The Tale of Princess Kaguya* that it would be difficult to recognise them as the work of the same director. His later films, in particular, rejected conventional anime styles, and he also approached the medium of animation as being far broader than traditional acetate cel work (although he was adept at using this process), unafraid to tackle new or radical techniques, such as the use of virtually drawn sketch frames imitating the style of ancient storybook prints, or using technology in *My Neighbours the Yamadas* to emphasise the cartoonish newsprint style of the original comics. This came at some cost in the time it took his projects to evolve. *The Tale of Princess Kaguya*, six years in the making, was meant to have double-billed with *The Wind Rises* but the delays in production meant that plan was halted.

In September 2013, Miyazaki announced his decision to retire from feature filmmaking. Despite announcing this after every film since *Princess Mononoke* (1997), he confirmed that *The Wind Rises* really was to be his final feature film. In August 2014, Suzuki Toshio made a statement indicating that production was likely to cease at the studio, at least for the time being. An internet uproar ensued as fans worldwide mourned the possible closure of the studio. However, their woes were a little premature. Like many studios, it is common practice to hire staff on contract for specific projects. Thanks to Ghibli's continuous production schedule that lasted over 25 years, the studio had always been active. However, following the release of *When Marnie Was There* (2014), there were no further feature films in production, so Suzuki took the opportunity to take stock and evaluate the studio's future. And Studio Ghibli was not to remain closed for long. Miyazaki once again came out of retirement and commenced production on a short film, *Boro the Caterpillar*, designed exclusively for the Ghibli Museum. He then announced in 2016 that he would be returning to feature film making with *How Do You Live?*, an adaptation of a 1937 novel by Genzaburō Yoshino, which initially had an estimated release date of 2020/2021, to coincide with the Tokyo Olympics. The studio opened up once more. In addition, Suzuki and Takahata took Dutch director Michaël Dudok de Wit under their respective wings to co-produce *The Red Turtle* (2016).

It was to be Takahata's last production. He was diagnosed with lung cancer and passed away on 5 April 2018 at the age of 82. Miyazaki mourned his friend at a ceremony that was held at the Ghibli Museum later that year. Takahata's legacy lies in a body of work that is innovative, intelligent and impassioned as well as demonstrating a sincere love of the animated form which inspired countless other filmmakers, not only within the studio that he helped found but also in his showcasing of animation from all over the world.

Miyazki worked on *How Do You Live?* for many years, without the constraints of a deadline. Release dates came and went. In the meantime, Miyazaki Gorō, Hayao's son, made Ghibli's first 3-D CGI feature, *Earwig and the Witch* (2020). Finally, and without any promotional material save a sole poster image, *How Do You Live?*, retitled *The Boy and the Heron* outside of Japan, was released in 2023, to much acclaim and the biggest box office opening weekend in Studio Ghibli's history.

Following the success of *The Boy and the Heron* thoughts turned to the studio's future. Nippon TV, who had had involvement with many of the studio's productions over the years, including *Ocean Waves* (1993), became the studio's largest shareholder in October 2023, turning Ghibli into a subsidiary. This marked a new era for the studio – what the future holds has yet to be seen.

THEMES AND MOTIFS

Many of the films of Studio Ghibli have common themes and motifs that make for a coherent worldview, even if the films themselves can be radically different in content or tone. Although the animations often share these common elements and usually a distinctive house aesthetic, they nevertheless retain the characteristics and interests of their respective directors.

Environmentalism

A key theme is that of environmentalism or, rather, the way that mankind interacts with nature, the way in which our environment is a living collection of interconnected beings that should be respected. Often Earth is portrayed as suffering as a result of human ignorance. What is particularly interesting is the way that this notion is explored from different angles and with different overall conclusions.

Nausicaä of the Valley of the Wind shows the devastating consequences of global pollution but also depicts groups of people who are still unwilling to take responsibility for their environment – using machinery to attempt to tame nature. Nausicaä herself is shown as trying, to the best of her ability, to understand the environment and live as harmoniously as she can within it. *My Neighbour Totoro* shows how respect for the environment can lead to harmony and reward, while its companion film, *Grave of the Fireflies*, shows the effect of war on a country. *Only Yesterday* (1991) depicts the gap between urban and country living and how the countryside is in decline through expanding wealth in an increasingly urbanised Japan. *Pom Poko* (1994) gives us just the tiniest glimpses of hope amidst a gloomy assessment of a natural environment in crisis. It posits that, in order for nature to have any chance of survival, it must adapt, even changing its very being. In *Ponyo on the Cliff by the Sea* (2008), the effects of consumption and the dumping of waste nearly prove to be Ponyo's downfall right at the start of the film as she becomes trapped in a discarded jar and has to escape being dredged up with all the debris on the seabed. Interestingly, though, it is also the fantasy world in *Ponyo* that can have a detrimental effect on Earth's environment – Ponyo's desire to become human, and her use of magic to metamorphose, upset the world's balance.

There is, however, a slight conflict in the way Ghibli debates the use of industrialism and machinery. In *Laputa: Castle in the Sky*, the mining village is seen as good because of its community work ethic, despite the fact that the residents are in some ways stealing from nature. Films featuring machinery in a good light acknowledge that it is inevitable that man and nature will have conflicting needs; it is more a question of how far humans are willing to tip the balance in order to fulfil their own selfish desires. Nausicaä may well be an environmentalist, but that doesn't stop her from using a flying vehicle to get around – the crucial difference being that hers represents the least damaging method of air travel, whereas the Pejitan and Tolmekian are depicted using huge, air-polluting warships. Similarly, in *Princess Mononoke*, the women who work in Lady Eboshi's factory are viewed as good community workers; it is what they are producing – weapons and iron – that places them in conflict with nature, for it is the deliberate destruction of the forest that is fuelling this new industrialism. Technology then, in and of itself, is not necessarily a bad thing, but we must consider how it's used and to what extent. In *Laputa: Castle in the Sky* the robots are destructive but also capable of living closely with nature, tending the gardens. Both *Laputa* and *Princess Mononoke* show us what begins to happen when nature can't coexist easily with humans. *Pom Poko* shows what happens when the battle, at least in some respects, is all but lost.

Flying

A running theme, particularly in Miyazaki Hayao's films, is the joy of flying and flying machines. Flying offers a freedom unrestricted by gravity and allows the animator to work in a completely uninhibited environment. This offers the possibility of exhilaration and speed in the animation. Flying machines appear frequently in Miyazaki's Ghibli and pre-Ghibli work, from the futuristic vehicles of *Conan, the Boy in Future*, the ornithopter in *The Castle of Cagliostro* and the wasp-like drones of *Laputa: Castle in the Sky* to the terrible warships of *Howl's Moving Castle* (2004) and the runaway dirigible of *Kiki's Delivery Service*. *Porco Rosso* (1992) is filled with aircraft, including the titular pig's crimson plane. A pig not dissimilar to *Porco Rosso*'s main character, Marco, introduces the wonderful contraptions in *Imaginary Flying Machines* (2002), a short film that played as part of Japan Airlines' (JAL) in-flight entertainment. *The Wind Rises* (2013) is about the (fictionalised) life of Horikoshi Jirō, a designer of Mitsubishi aircraft.

Similarly, the fantastical worlds of Studio Ghibli are filled with flying creatures – Totoro, the Baron from *Whisper of the Heart* (1995) and *The Cat Returns* (2002), the huge insects of *Nausicaä of the Valley of the Wind* or the dragons from *Tales from Earthsea* (2006) and *Spirited Away*. What is interesting about these creatures is the way that they interact with the humans in the story, serving as a metaphor for growing up or showing that sometimes freedom comes at a price. Often, as with Totoro or the Baron, they fly with the human characters to show them the world from a different perspective.

Children

A child or young adult functions as the central protagonist of many Ghibli films. This serves a number of purposes. Children are more open to the kind of fantastical worlds that are often portrayed, as in *Spirited Away* and *The Boy and the Heron*. Children are spirited and resourceful, more likely to face up to grave danger willingly because they have not yet developed the faculties to recognise threat, or are even excited by it. Mimi in *Panda Kopanda* is one such character, delighted with the thought that the intruder in her home could be an actual burglar! Similarly, a group of schoolgirls are thrilled to be captured by pirates in *Porco Rosso* – and go on to disrupt their dastardly deeds. Related to this is the sense of a child's vulnerability in the face of adversity – it makes the tension more palpable to the viewer.

In many ways, the children in Ghibli's films are a liberating force that allows anything to be possible. Having a child as a main character gives a younger audience a greater identification with the film, but also functions as an avatar for adult wish fulfilment, offering possibilities for a return to youth. The child has a privileged viewpoint that sees what an adult can't, or won't, see – for example, Shizuku's observation of the cat that sits in her train carriage in *Whisper of the Heart* or the two sisters who can see the forest spirits in *My Neighbour*

Totoro. Sometimes the child is used as a way of observing adult atrocities through younger eyes – such as the poison blighting the land in *Princess Mononoke*, the bombing of Kōbe in *Grave of the Fireflies* or the terrible war in *Howl's Moving Castle*. Indeed, Howl himself embodies many of these characteristics with his initial unwillingness to grow up and accept responsibility.

Anthropomorphism, Zoomorphism and Metamorphosis

Anthropomorphism – animals adopting human characteristics – is a staple feature in animation, but the way Ghibli uses it is far more subtle than, say, the cute talking animals of Disney. Linked with this is zoomorphism – characters having the form of an animal. The balance between these is a key aspect of many of Ghibli's films and often indicates shifts in character and meaning, especially when combined with the process of metamorphosis.

In the pre-Ghibli *Gōshu the Cellist*, Takahata anthropomorphises the animals who visit Gōshu nightly but they do retain their individual animal traits even as they converse or plead with the cellist. The relationships between forms are more subtle in *Pom Poko* where the level of anthropomorphism alters depending on the *tanuki*'s (raccoon-dogs') state of mind, developing from realistic depictions, through stylised manifestations right up to full-scale transformation into human form, a form that at once shows the extent of their powers but also the lengths they need to go to in order to survive in the human world. The depiction of the grey heron in *The Boy and the Heron* is initially highly realistic but becomes increasingly fluid as we discover that the heron's body is actually inhabited by a small man. In *Kiki's Delivery Service*, Jiji the cat is notably feline but can converse openly with Kiki. Cats take human form through the figure of the Baron in *Whisper of the Heart* and also in the world of the Cat King in *The Cat Returns*. Anthropomorphism is taken to its limit in films like *Spirited Away* and *Tales from Earthsea*, where characters appear to be human, only to be revealed later as dragons adopting human form.

It isn't just a question of animals taking on human traits, but also of humans becoming like animals. *Porco Rosso*'s Marco has zoomorphised into a bipedal pig and it is implied that this was a conscious decision on his part to remove himself from the rest of humanity. More directly, Chihiro's parents' greed in *Spirited Away* causes them to turn into devouring swine. Princess Mononoke doesn't physically take on the looks of the wolves she runs with, but adopts their mannerisms and habits. With anthropomorphism in Ghibli's films, the change is normally seen as either a conscious choice or part of the animal's natural ability. In the case of zoomorphism, however, characters often have change thrust upon them through magic, circumstance or curses.

Metamorphosis is a vital element in many Ghibli films, either through deliberate use of magic to alter form (Yubāba in *Spirited Away*, Howl in *Howl's Moving Castle*) or through the effects of mankind (the poisoned boar-god in *Princess Mononoke*). Metamorphosis is used to visually represent a character's emotions, state of mind or well-being. Sophie in *Howl's Moving Castle* is not only transformed into an old woman magically; in a crucial sense, the change is also brought about by her own lack of self-confidence. Similarly, Ponyo's grasp of her magical ability to will herself into human form in *Ponyo on the Cliff by the Sea* manifests itself in her appearance, but also reflects the level of her fatigue and emotional state. In *The Boy and the Heron* Miyazaki's depiction of the characters is highly sophisticated as we see younger incarnations of some of the protagonists in the other world.

Wind and Weather

Climate plays an important role for aesthetic, emotional or thematic reasons. The state of the weather and its relationship to the environment demonstrates the delicate balances in nature – the electric storms and desert wastelands of the ravaged Earth in *Nausicaä of the Valley of the Wind*, the heavy drops of rain in *Grave of the Fireflies* or the terrifying tsunami in *Ponyo on the Cliff by the Sea*. Moreover, the weather is often used to reflect the characters' feelings – Mei and Satsuki's despondent wait at the bus stop in *My Neighbour Totoro* is accompanied by a torrential downpour while a (short-lived) feeling of utter contentment is greeted by glorious sunshine as Haru relaxes in a field in *The Cat Returns*.

Weather helps create a more immersive experience for the audience as well as showing the true art of the animator. The wind causes undulating waves in the grass and wheat fields, conveying the weather visually and creating a more believable environment that increases the overall impact of the film. Similarly, wind is visualised when it blows through characters' hair or causes their clothing to billow and flap – in particular, the flying sequences in *Kiki's Delivery Service* and *Laputa: Castle in the Sky* feel more realistic because of this. Marco's choice of a scarf in *Porco Rosso* allows the animators to give a greater impression of speed as he flies because, unlike Kiki, Marco does not have a full head of hair. And the wind is the catalyst for Jirō and Naoko meeting in *The Wind Rises*, in the aftermath of the Great Kanto Earthquake of 1923.

Worlds Within Our Own

Ghibli's fantasy films often evoke the notion of worlds that exist within our own but of which we are oblivious. The sense of wonder, or even fear, gained from glimpses of these other worlds is normally seen through the eyes of young adults, children or the very old. There is a very real sense that the rationality of adulthood is incapable of viewing the fantastical and spiritual in our midst because it is blinded by logic and reason. In *Howl's Moving Castle*, Sophie sees many lands, beautiful and terrifying, through the eyes, not just of a young adult, but also an old woman.

> *'Happily he is the second time come to them. For they say an old man is twice a child.' Hamlet* (II.2.385)

The relationship of adults to these other worlds is perhaps most clearly spelt out in the portrayal of that most sympathetic of adults, Kusakabe Tatsuo in *My Neighbour Totoro*. He never tries to deny his daughters their imaginations or insight into other worlds, but it is implied that, as a rational adult, he has no access to these worlds himself. In contrast, Kanta's grandmother, having overshot adulthood, has a closer relationship to the world of Totoro and the woodland spirits. Totoro's forest is one of many coexisting worlds in Ghibli's films, ranging from the horrific parallel world in *Spirited Away*, the alternate worlds with multiple iterations of the characters in *The Boy and the Heron* to the hedonistic partying of the *tanuki* in *Pom Poko*. The coexistence of the spirit and mortal worlds is more visible in *Princess Mononoke*, which depicts a time when the two worlds are becoming increasingly distinguished from each other. In feudal Japan, humans lived in harmony with the natural world, but the development of industrialism has polluted the lands of the ancient gods and created conflict. Mononoke herself represents this moving away from a universe of mutual coexistence to one where the spirit world tries to sever ties with the human world in order to survive. Ghibli films normally show characters from the real world entering the fantastical, but in *Ponyo on the Cliff by the Sea* it is the unseen world that crashes into ours when Ponyo escapes her ocean-bound confines.

These worlds within worlds do not need to exist physically; they can reside purely in the imagination. In *Whisper of the Heart*, Shizuku is taken on a whirlwind tour of a fantastical land by the Baron, a character in the book she will eventually write. Contrast this with the film's semi-sequel *The Cat Returns*, and the world of the Baron is very much a real one, reached via a portal. It is part of the world around us, but hidden in tiny plazas and places that adult minds just do not comprehend.

Japanese Mythology

Closely linked to environmental concerns is Shintō, Japan's indigenous religion, which, until the US occupation in 1945, was a part of state affairs, directly linking the emperor to the gods. Ghibli's films do not explicitly refer to Shintō but its customs are enshrined within Japanese culture. Shintō is at heart an animistic religion that sees gods and spirits in everything, resulting in a respect for human harmony with the natural environment. *Jinja* (shrines) and their *torii* (sacred gates) can be seen in many Ghibli films and Shintō customs depicted include paying respect at shrines or leaving offerings. *Kami* are the spirits that reside in all things. *Princess Mononoke* is filled with *kami*, from the powerful forest god Shishigami to the little clicking *kodama*. The term *kami* can encompass many things and *kami* may have various other names depending on their form.

In Japanese mythology, *obake* are spirits that have the ability to transform. Creatures can often metamorphose into various forms, sometimes human – like the *kitsune* (foxes) and *tanuki* in *Pom Poko*. There are also *yōkai* – odd and varied spirits that can be anything from an ogre to a *karakasa*, a one-eyed, one-legged umbrella with a lolling tongue (see *Pom Poko*) – and *oni* (demons). Dragons are also part of Japanese mythology, although they derive partly from Buddhist legends.

Buddhism is Japan's second-largest religion with many Japanese people considering themselves followers of both Buddhism *and* Shintō. Buddhist images appear in a number of Ghibli's films, notably *Pom Poko* and *My Neighbour Totoro*, which features *jizō* statues, as well as the conclusion to *The Tale of Princess Kaguya*, which features the Amida Butsu descending on a cloud to take the princess home. Often to be found at the roadside or near graveyards, these are seen as guardians who protect children.

Social Community

Both Takahata and Miyazaki were prominent members of the workers' unions at Tōei studios and their commitment to social justice is apparent in the communities that populate their films. These communities are shown as collectively aiming for a common goal and making the best of things. From the villagers of the pre-Ghibli *Horusu: Prince of the Sun* to the working women's collective in *Princess Mononoke* and the miners in *Laputa: Castle in the Sky*, all face threats from the establishment, either through war, industrialism or attempted dictatorship. Similarly, the Valley of the Wind tribe in *Nausicaä* gathers together for the greater good, surviving by working as a community rather than as individuals.

> *'Here, you see, are two kinds of work – one good, the other bad; one not far removed from a blessing, a lightening of life; the other a mere curse, a burden to life.' Useful Work versus Useless Toil* by William Morris

In Ghibli's 'hands-on' approach to animation as a craft, there is a John Ruskin-like sense of the nobility of craftsmanship over industrialism, or, as Morris puts it, 'Useful Work versus Useless Toil'. This is further reflected in the agricultural work of social pioneer Miyazawa Kenji, author of *Gōshu the Cellist*. Miyazawa fought to keep communities together by improving farming methods in order to relieve poverty, as well as culturally enriching people's lives through his gently moralistic tales. Nausicaä's conflict between technological survival and natural survival can be seen in these environmentally socialist terms. So too can Gōshu's honest art as a cellist, the violin maker in *Whisper of the Heart*, the bread-making and artistry in *Kiki's Delivery Service* or Fio and the ladies repairing a battered old plane in *Porco Rosso*. All of these are forms of social craft that improve the lives and health of the people who practise them and the people who benefit from them. In *Spirited Away*, Chihiro's parents' consumerist attitude literally turns them into pigs. Sharing reaps rewards in *My Neighbour Totoro* but selfishness and pride lead to despair in *Grave of the Fireflies*. Takahata's *Only Yesterday* has its characters actively debate the gap between rural and urban dwellers. Taeko's middle-class city spinster's life is transformed when she finally gets a chance to visit the countryside. Once there, an initially bitter and sceptical Toshio explains to her the struggles of daily life. But, through her honest work, Taeko begins to gain a true sense of social understanding and the benefits of community living over isolated life in an overpopulated city. These are not just the idealistic aspirations of political dreamers. In his documentary *The Story of the Yanagawa Canals* (1987), Takahata shows how social and environmental collaboration can have a real and beneficial impact on communities.

European Influences

The influence of European locations is notable in a number of the films. Many of the pre-Ghibli TV series that Takahata and Miyazaki worked on had European sources, including *Heidi, a Girl of the Alps* (1974) and *A Dog of Flanders* (1975). Research trips for these series as well as for an aborted *Pippi Longstocking* project still feed into much of the architecture seen in the Ghibli films that are not set in Japan, notably the Scandinavian town setting of *Kiki's Delivery Service* and the Mediterranean islands of *Porco Rosso*. The mining town of *Laputa: Castle in the Sky* was inspired by visits Miyazaki made to Wales in the 1980s. *Howl's Moving Castle* and *Earwig and the Witch* were both based on novels by Diana Wynne Jones and are set in British locations, the latter of which is very specific. In *Whisper of the Heart*, the pull of Europe's tradition of making classical instruments sees Seiji trying to realise a dream of studying violin making in Cremona, Italy. In *The Cat Returns*, the hidden part of the real world where the Baron lives is clearly modelled on European market squares. And, although an adaptation of *Pippi Longstocking* was not to be, Astrid Lindgren's *Ronja, the Robber's Daughter* (2014) would be produced as a TV series directed by Miyazaki Gorō. Some films, however, despite the source material originating in Europe, transpose the setting to Japan. *Arrietty*, based on the English novel *The Borrowers*, was set in a grand old Japanese house instead of an English country home.

Japanese Culture

Part of the joy in watching Studio Ghibli films is their 'Japaneseness', even in films set ostensibly in a European context. Despite the influence of the West on Japanese culture, Japan is a society that has managed to retain its customs, practices, food, clothing and etiquette even in the face of world corporate hegemony. While a working understanding of Japanese culture is not necessary to enjoy the films, some familiarity is essential in order to understand their finer points. Apart from aspects of Japanese mythology mentioned above, there are a plethora of associated customs that help explain character motivation and elements of the films that some Western commentators seem to find uncomfortable. *My Neighbour Totoro* and *Only Yesterday* are cases in point. In *My Neighbour Totoro*, when Mei, Satsuki and their father enjoy a relaxing bath together it is a sign of family harmony. Bathing is a traditional Japanese way of relaxing, distinct from washing, which is performed prior to bathing, so as not to dirty the bathwater. In *Only Yesterday*, Taeko has her fondest memories recalling her trip to an *onsen*, naturally hot springs of mineral-rich water, on her only previous trip to the countryside. In *My Neighbour Totoro*, Satsuki scuttles inside their new house on her knees to ensure that her shoes don't touch the floor, a significant cultural taboo. Although she is following the letter of the protocol, she is not really following the spirit, marking the scene as innocently humorous. In *Only Yesterday*, failure to remove her shoes indoors results in Taeko receiving a slap from her father.

Japanese school life features in a number of Ghibli films, showing practices ranging from group physical education exercises known as radio taisō in *Only Yesterday* to Japanese school festivals in *Ocean Waves*. Pupils are responsible for cleaning their own classrooms, which is why you see them doing so in *Ocean Waves* and *Whisper of the Heart*. *Ocean Waves* also makes mention of Japan's notorious cram schools where underachieving pupils spend their summers desperately trying to stuff themselves full of information in order to get a good university place. In *From Up On Poppy Hill* (2011) Matsuzaki Umi's school life is integral to her development and burgeoning relationship as she becomes involved with the school magazine and the renovation of the school club house.

Food is an important part of Japanese society. Many of the characters eat with incredible gusto – from Lupin's recuperation gluttony in the pre-Ghibli *The Castle of Cagliostro* to the breakfast shenanigans in *Howl's Moving Castle*, from the feasts of *Porco Rosso* to Ponyo devouring Sōsuke's ham and her enthusiastic *ramen* (noodle) slurping. Umi conscientiously prepares breakfast and dinner for the boarding house guests in *From Up on Poppy Hill*. Often the food is instantly recognisable, but, in many cases, the brands or foodstuffs on show are less familiar in the West. The traditional hard candies in a can, Sakuma Drops, are a long-established brand and feature extensively in *Grave of the Fireflies*, while Lisa drinks Sapporo beer in *Ponyo on the Cliff by the Sea*. *Umeboshi* (sour salted plums), *okonomiyaki* (a cross between a pancake and a pizza), *yakitori* (grilled skewered chicken) and *bento* (lunch boxes) all make appearances. A travelling food stall in *Pom Poko* keeps two drunken salarymen from being aware of the chaos around them. *My Neighbours the Yamadas* is packed with food references, which usually stem from attempts by Mrs Yamada to avoid work as much as possible – like tricking her son into making her *ramen* or providing her husband with a proper Japanese breakfast, cobbled together from leftovers.

Trains are an intrinsic part of Japanese life – partly because the rail infrastructure is extensive and efficient, but also because road transport, for many, is expensive and not terribly convenient. Trains play a vital role in Ghibli films – they are consistently seen as beneficial, taking their protagonists on metaphysical as well as literal journeys. Taeko takes a trip back to her childhood on a train journey in *Only Yesterday*, Chihiro has a surreal ride in *Spirited Away*, Naoko and Jirō meet on a train in *The Wind Rises*, and Shizuku's eventful rail journey with a cat is the catalyst for events in *Whisper of the Heart*.

EXPLANATORY NOTES

Japanese names are expressed surname first followed by given name.

Titles in this book are given with their preferred English title, that is, the title given by Ghibli, if there is one, or a translated one if not. For example, the film *Ocean Waves* was the title eventually announced by Studio Ghibli for their rarely seen television movie. Prior to this it was known under the translated title *I Can Hear the Sea*. A Japanese transliteration of the title is also provided so that each film can be identified if there is some debate about the translated title.

Almost all of Studio Ghibli's films are available in dubbed form. All the reviews and comments in this book are based upon the original Japanese versions of the films. As such, and due to the vagaries of translation, direct quotes from the films may differ slightly from those you are familiar with.

We discuss each film in detail, so please be warned that, if you haven't seen that title yet, there may be spoilers in the commentary.

THE PRE-GHIBLI WORKS OF TAKAHATA ISAO AND MIYAZAKI HAYAO

Studio Ghibli did not form in a vacuum. Both Takahata Isao and Miyazaki Hayao had a number of jobs with different animation companies before they finally formed their own studio. The pair had worked on a large number of productions of various sizes and in many different roles. This section will concentrate on the major television series Miyazaki and Takahata worked on as well as all their theatrical releases as directors prior to the formation of Studio Ghibli.

THE TŌEI YEARS

Both Takahata and Miyazaki began their careers working in the factory-like animation studios at Tōei Dōga. Tōei produced TV series as well as feature films and the pair worked on both, their paths crossing on several projects, notably on the series *Wolf Boy Ken* (1964-5). In general, Takahata's role in the early years at Tōei was as assistant director while Miyazaki progressed from in-betweening work through to key animation (including a couple of episodes of the popular series *Sally the Witch* [1966-8]) and eventually design. The pair's biggest project at Tōei, *Horusu, Prince of the Sun*, was an artistic triumph but a commercial failure. Takahata would not direct another feature for the company and returned to television work. Miyazaki, meanwhile, continued his involvement with animated features, contributing to such films as *Puss 'n Boots* (1969) and *The Flying Ghost Ship* (1969), the latter featuring a scene in which a giant robot devastates a city, foreshadowing *Laputa: Castle in the Sky*. *Puss 'n Boots* is particularly striking in its use of design and perspective, combining comic *kawaii* (cute) characters and quirky action sequences. With a princess to rescue, a castle with a dungeon full of skulls and bones and a daring rescue, it's chock-full of sequences that anticipate Miyazaki's later *The Castle of Cagliostro*. As a tie-in to the film Miyazaki also drew a serialised manga version of the tale. *Treasure Island* (aka *Animal Treasure Island*, 1971) retold Robert Louis Stevenson's classic story as a madcap adventure with much of the cast as animals, most notably the pirates of the ship *Pork Saute*, who are pigs. Even more crazy was *Ali Baba and the 40 Thieves* (1971), a sequel to the familiar story where Ali Baba's descendant is now an evil tyrant and the 'thieves' are actually the good guys – Al Huck and a bunch of cats and a rat – seeking to topple the King.

POST-TŌEI

Both Miyazaki and Takahata quit Tōei to find work elsewhere. An attempt in 1971 to film *Pippi Longstocking* was put on hold when the author Astrid Lindgren declined to grant rights to the books. Their first major project was on the television series *Lupin III* (1971), based upon the hilarious but vulgar manga by Monkey Punch, for which they both took directing credits. Although not as racy as the manga, the series was notably bawdier than the film that later became Miyazaki's directorial feature debut and which was taken from the same source material. Miyazaki would also find himself directing two episodes for the second series in 1980. Other small television jobs followed but the public craze for pandas in the 1970s led to the theatrical release of the short film *Panda Kopanda*, directed by Takahata with story, design and animation by Miyazaki. Further television work followed but the two really hit their stride with *Heidi, a Girl of the Alps*.

THE NIPPON ANIMATION YEARS

Although it underwent a number of title changes and company rebrandings over the years, Nippon Animation's *World Masterpiece Theater* was a prodigious production. From 1969, the company aimed to produce annually an animated version of a classic story, which was serialised weekly, with some of the titles running to a full 52 weeks. Miyazaki had previously worked on the series' adaptation of *Moomin* (1969-70). *Heidi, a Girl of the Alps* (*Arupusu no Shōjo Haiji*, 1974), directed by Takahata and with Miyazaki handling design, was a huge success with its charming characters and attention to detail, particularly in the animation of the animals. Based upon the popular nineteenth-century books by Swiss author Johanna Spyri, *Heidi* is the tale of an orphaned girl living with her grandfather in the Alps. The use of sweeping scenery, the careful pacing and the vivid animation made the show a hit, and it was syndicated abroad. It was so successful that a feature film was released, edited from episodes of the series.

Both Miyazaki and Takahata worked briefly on *A Dog of Flanders* (*Furandāsu no Inu*, 1975), based on the classic novel by Ouida (Maria Louise de la Ramée), but returned to larger-scale productions with *From the Apennines to the Andes* (aka *3,000 Ri to Visit Mother, Haha o Tazunete Sanzen-ri*, 1976). The hero of the story is Marco, who is living in Italy in the late nineteenth century. His mother works in Argentina to send money to the family, but when the regular letters she sends her son stop arriving, Marco takes it upon himself to get to the root of the problem, leading to an epic journey across continents.

Once again Takahata was responsible for directing the series and Miyazaki for design, the result being another success, spawning a belated theatrical release edited from the series in 1980. Various jobs on other *World Masterpiece Theater* productions followed, including *Rascal the Raccoon* (*Araiguma Rasukaru* 1977). The pair's final major work for the series was *Anne of Green Gables* (*Red-haired Anne*, *Akage no An*, 1979) from the book by Canadian writer LM Montgomery. Takahata directed the series and Miyazaki worked on the earlier episodes before leaving Nippon Animation. The exceptional backgrounds and realistic animation mark this as a superior TV series. Anne is an orphan girl who grows up in her adoptive parents' home, Green Gables, and endears herself to them, despite them having wanted a boy. A gentle animation, as well as an accurate adaptation of its source, the series illustrated Takahata's growing interest in the boundaries between childhood and adulthood, which would come to mark much of his later work. Takahata constantly looks at the growing-up process and the way in which children tackle their increasing responsibilities.

Prior to *Anne of Green Gables* Miyazaki had been working on another project for Nippon Animation, but not as part of *World Masterpiece Theater*. *Conan, the Boy in Future* (1978), an adaptation of Alexander Key's *The Incredible Tide*, was an ambitious and exciting adventure epic that signalled the real genesis of Miyazaki's style as a director. Miyazaki designed, storyboarded and directed nearly all 26 episodes with the help of Takahata (storyboards) and their mentor Ōtsuka Yasuo (animation director). The importance of this landmark series is difficult to overemphasise. Like many Miyazaki productions it appears to be aimed predominantly at the youth market, yet it contains nuances and perspectives that transcend the bland entertainment often passed off as family viewing.

Set in 2008, young Conan mistakenly believes that he and his grandfather, plunged back on to a dying world when their spaceship fails to escape the atmosphere, are the last of the human race, the other survivors of this terrible crash having since died. The world's oceans have risen and the Earth has been ravaged by a terrible war that has turned it into a devastated wasteland. Out shark-hunting one day, Conan chances upon Lana, a pretty girl whose grandfather could hold the key to mankind's salvation. Unfortunately, the military island Industria, seeking world domination, want the secrets and stop at nothing to get them, kidnapping Lana in hopes of getting to her grandfather. After his grandfather is killed, Conan embarks upon a quest, aided by oddball companions he meets along the way, to save Lana and, potentially, the planet. The links to the natural world, the *Nausicaä*-like, post-apocalyptic scenario and the similarities in design to *Laputa: Castle in the Sky* all point to Miyazaki's future work. The series delights in scenes of flying and imaginary vehicles – in episode two, Conan bravely tries to rescue Lana from one such flying machine, using his harpoon to pry it open like a tin can. Themes relating to the resilience and hope of the young, the nature of friendship and community, the stupidity of warring nations and the relationship between people and the environment all feature heavily. The ideas of communicating with animals, of psychic links and of peoples isolated from each other all feed into later projects, and there are even underwater scenes that recall works such as the Ghibli Museum short film *Water Spider Monmon* (2006) and *Ponyo on the Cliff by the Sea*. Considering the series was destined for television (it was eventually syndicated but never received an English-language release), the quality of the animation, like most of Nippon Animation's output, is staggering. The characters, in particular, are portrayed with great flexibility: realistic in the serious scenes, deliberately stylised during the more comic moments that help temper the otherwise grave journey.

One curious quirk (one that is common for TV anime) is the short comic sequence that marks the advertising break halfway through the episode. *Conan, the Boy in Future*'s repeating motif is a series of body match cards that feature the characters and creatures of the show, so that, for example, Conan might temporarily find himself with a shark's tail instead of legs. Many of the staff who worked on *Conan, the Boy in Future* would eventually find their way onto the payroll of Studio Ghibli.

POST-NIPPON ANIMATION

After leaving Nippon Animation, Miyazaki was plunged headfirst into his first feature film as a director – the madcap caper *Lupin III: Castle of Cagliostro*. Takahata, meanwhile, was continuing his own career as a director with the comic *Downtown Story* and the delightful *Gōshu the Cellist*. Although he had worked on a number of TV projects, Miyazaki's most successful work post-*Conan* came with six episodes of *Sherlock Hound* (*Meitantei Houmuzu*, 1982). This Italian-Japanese co-production retells Conan Doyle's Sherlock Holmes stories through the conceit of using anthropomorphised dogs in the majority of the roles. The end result has beautifully realised Victorian settings and transport but the action scenes really push the animation to its limits. The anachronistic use of technology (there are early planes as well as steamships and trains that are familiar in design but deliberately not quite based on real vehicles) gives the series a distinct aesthetic that is striking and effective. Although the series suffered legal problems initially, it did eventually get released and proved highly successful.

Both Miyazaki and Takahata spent time working on the expensive and long-delayed film of *Little Nemo* (1982-89), a huge multinational co-production that really showed what cutting-edge animation could achieve, given the resources. However, both resigned from the troubled production, which had already seen a number of personnel changes and rewrites even before their involvement. Miyazaki returned to directing with his second feature film, the eco-epic *Nausicaä of the Valley of the Wind*, and its unprecedented success led to the formation of Studio Ghibli.

Horusu: Prince of the Sun/The Little Norse Prince (Taiyō no Ōji: Horusu no Daibōken) (1968)

Directed by: Takahata Isao

Plucky boy warrior Horusu should be enjoying a simple life in his peaceful village but malevolent would-be dictator Grunwald unleashes savage silver wolves to attack the community and scatter its people. Brave Horusu plucks the Sword of the Sun from the arm of Mogue, a gargantuan rock man, and is given the task of reuniting his oppressed compatriots, a feat he can only aohiovo by roforging the blade and becoming the legendary Prince of the Sun. As if the villagers did not have enough to contend with, there's also a giant killer pike that's gobbling up the fishermen, a rat invasion and the prospect of further evil creatures conjured from the depths of Grunwald's black soul. Horusu does have aid in the shape of his companion Koro, an enthusiastic bear cub. Less clear are the motives of Chiro, a chirpy squirrel, deeply suspicious owl, Toto, and melancholy singer, Hilda, cursed by her own solitude. Horusu must decide whether he should reforge the sword that could fulfil his destiny.

Horusu: Prince of the Sun was the first feature film directed by Takahata Isao and one that would mark a defining moment in Japanese animation. Despite its mythical setting in Scandinavia (allegedly the setting was changed at the behest of the Tōei bosses who were unhappy that the film was to centre on the Ainu people of Japan), the film is a reflection of the political and social struggles of the time. The feeling at Tōei just then was that they were treated less as artists and more like factory workers, churning out kids' cartoons rather than films with a deeper purpose. *Horusu* was produced by Takahata and many from the Tōei union team, including Miyazaki and future character designer on *The Castle of Cagliostro* and *Conan, the Boy in Future*, Ōtsuka Yasuo, to show that an adventure film could have a social context. What is so striking about *Horusu* is the way that it mixes a rip-roaring tale of heroism with vivid, openly socialist content. The village is like a cooperative, the villagers happy in their work. The simplistic rural lifestyle is seen as wholesome and would later be reflected in films like *Only Yesterday* and *Pom Poko*. In these later films, socialism is a notable but subtle subtext; in *Horusu* the links are more blatant – Horusu himself often being portrayed from a low angle as a people's hero. Most strikingly, the scenes where the Sword of the Sun is finally forged are produced in a style that recalls Sergei Eisenstein and Dziga Vertov.

At heart *Horusu* is a mythic adventure, full of epic battles, betrayals and heroic deeds. What is interesting about some of Takahata and Miyazaki's projects is the influence of European stories and myths, albeit told from a distinctly Japanese perspective. In *Horusu*, aspects of Norse mythology and Arthurian tales of swords in stones, sorcery and destiny are particularly apparent.

Without the budget to sustain a fully animated feature-length animation (that is, animating 24 frames per second of film), *Horusu* employs a number of techniques to make its tale appear as expansive as possible. Ōtsuka Yasuo had previously experimented with fully animating key sequences and virtually ignoring the animation on others, making the film stylistically varied and interesting but more frugal. In *Horusu*, establishing shots of the village or montage sequences, such as the rat invasion, are shown as a series of static pictures, rostrum camera panned to give some sense of movement. At other moments the full animation is breathtaking, the beautiful sketched outlines of Horusu himself intricate and dynamic. The scene of Horusu at sea, as perfectly animated Hokusai-inspired waves crash around him, is a true highpoint for the art form. Despite the intentions of the filmmakers not to produce anything too sanitised or specifically like Disney, *Horusu* nevertheless contains many elements that are closer to Disney than almost anything else they produced, albeit the Disney that created its most glorious, financially unsuccessful follies. It's difficult to see Grunwald towering over the village without being reminded of 'Night on Bald Mountain' from *Fantasia* (1940), or the animals from *Sleeping Beauty* (1959). The abundant anthropomorphised animals in *Horusu*, although often cute, never stray into the territory of being annoying. Indeed, their closely observed movements, particularly those of Koro the bear and Chiro the squirrel, appear to be dry runs for Takahata's wonderful *Gōshu the Cellist*.

Horusu: Prince of the Sun is a triumph of animation filmmaking, an epic adventure with a socially conscious heart. Unfortunately for Takahata, the film failed to set the box office alight despite the artistry on show, although it has since been seen as pivotal in the history of cel animation as an art form. Tōei's initial reaction was to castigate its staff for wasting their time and money. Facing a more restrictive future, Takahata, Miyazaki and Ōtsuka eventually left the studio.

Panda Kopanda (1972) & *Panda Kopanda and the Rainy Day Circus (Panda Kopanda: Amefuri Saakasu no Maki)* (1973)

Directed by: Takahata Isao
Written by: Miyazaki Hayao

After seeing her grandmother off at the local train station, Mimiko faces the prospect of life on her own with determination and some excitement – after all, if she's *really* lucky, she could meet some actual burglars. Instead of regular criminals, though, Mimiko finds a cute baby panda and its imposing father munching on the bamboo shoots close to her house. She instantly takes them to her heart and they become a little family. However, domestic bliss proves ephemeral when a reward for recapturing the missing pandas creates a hunt for the pair.

In *Amefuri Saakasu no Maki (Rainy Circus)* the reunited trio find themselves in the company of another child, a destructive but delightful creature, the Tigger-like tiger Tiny, whose trick is turning on the tip of his tail. Matters turn from cute domestic antics to more serious concerns when a massive rainstorm threatens to flood the area. Tiny's real mother is trapped in a circus cage, and the waters are rising rapidly...

Panda Kopanda arrived at a fortuitous time. China's often strained relationship with Japan had relaxed, symbolised through the gift of two diplomatic emissaries from Beijing: Ran Ran and Kan Kan, a pair of adorable pandas. The stampede to see these black-and-white beauties took the authorities so much by surprise that riot police had to be called in to curb the crowds at Ueno Park Zoo. Arriving at the peak of this pandamonium (if you will) *Panda Kopanda* (*Panda, Baby Panda*) is certainly a reflection of the times – Mimiko's squeals of delight and celebratory handstands are reflective of the hysteria that greeted Ran Ran and Kan Kan. At heart, *Panda Kopanda*, despite its *joie de vivre* and childlike sense of adventure, is about childhood loneliness dispelled by imagination and wonder, and also the freedom that creatures need in order to be themselves. Rather than celebrating the pandas' real-life cousins, the film actually denounces their treatment; when Papa Panda is asked what a zoo is, his reply is 'a place where there are no nice bamboo groves'.

Mimiko represents the spirit of young people; determined, ever cheerful and distinctly unmodern, she doesn't even have a TV, so is unaware that her new adopted family are escapees. Although she is independent enough to live on her own while her grandmother is away, her good nature ensures that everyone else in her small community is keeping a watchful eye on her. The adoption of both a father and a son (the theme song repeats the line 'panda, papa panda, baby panda' to indicate that, in some sense, they are the family she has created) gives her responsibility and protection in an unconventional family environment.

Both *Panda Kopanda* films show the very collaborative process of animation, with direction by Takahata and story by Miyazaki. Also on board was Ōtsuka Yasuo as animation director. There is little doubt that it is Miyazaki's quirky view of the childhood spirit that is coming through in this film, with many story and design elements cropping up in his later works. The clearest relationship is with *My Neighbour Totoro*, the large Papa Panda possessing a mighty bellow to go with his rotund figure. Panny is forced to act like a stuffed toy when taken to school, echoing Jiji's rigid mimicry of a toy cat in *Kiki's Delivery Service*, while the scenes by the river, particularly those involving a nose-nipping lobster, pre-date the similar style of *Water Spider Monmon*.

Panda Kopanda and its sequel offer simple, innocent pleasure and humour combined with an infectiously chirpy theme song.

Lupin the Third: The Castle of Cagliostro (Rupan Sansei: Kariosutoro no Shiro) (1979)

Directed by: Miyazaki Hayao

After a daring casino raid, master thief and debonair playboy Lupin, together with his trusty companion Jigen, are forced to dump the spoils of their larceny when it becomes clear that their haul consists entirely of 'goat bills', exceptionally realistic counterfeit money allegedly manufactured in the Duchy of Cagliostro. The dodgy duo attempt to save Princess Clarisse from a determined bunch of bowler-hatted scallywags who are working for the Grand Duke of Cagliostro, but they fail to do so. Clarisse is to be married to the evil Duke who believes the union of two sides of the family will reveal untold wealth. Lupin is determined to break into the castle – after all, the prospect of getting the money *and* the girl is too good an opportunity to miss – but the combination of labyrinthine dungeons, lasers, trapdoors and an elite guard of metal-clawed ninja (Shadows) means it's not going to be easy. With occasional help from Fujiko, a feisty combat-trained reporter and ex-flame, mysterious swordsman Goemon and even a begrudging policeman, Inspector Zenigata of Interpol, Lupin and Jigen aim to put an end to the Duke's nefarious nuptial plans.

Arsène Lupin, detective and 'gentleman thief', is the celebrated creation of French author Maurice Leblanc. The character first appeared in 1905, apparently as a response to the worldwide success of Sir Arthur Conan Doyle's Sherlock Holmes. *Lupin III* follows the adventures of Lupin's grandson – less of a gentleman, more of a thief – in a series of exaggerated adventures created by mangaka Katō Kazuhiko, aka Monkey Punch. Lupin's increasingly outlandish schemes and tendency towards being on the receiving end of much punishment is compounded by his insatiable libido and uncontrollable lasciviousness. The manga became a huge success and was turned into an animated TV series in 1971. Both Takahata and Miyazaki worked extensively on this first series, directing a large proportion of the episodes. This was to mark Miyazaki's first credited work as a director. When animation director Ōtsuka Yasuo was looking at producing a second feature-film spin-off (the first being *The Mystery of Mamo* [1978]) he turned to Miyazaki who set about rewriting the story, with Yamazaki Haruya, for his feature-film debut. Although the opportunity finally to break out on to the big screen was enticing, the actualities of creating this breathtakingly inventive film were far from ideal – the team had just five months to deliver it. Fortunately, the pressures of television animation had given Miyazaki the ability to manage this punishing workload. Unfortunately, the pace of production meant that some of Miyazaki's ideas were left on the drawing board. Interestingly, Lupin is still a ladies' man but far less lecherous than his manga and small-screen counterparts and with good reason. Lupin's extreme foibles work better in an episodic medium where you get to like the character over time. For a standalone feature, Miyazaki had to establish audience identification with what is essentially an anti-hero early on, so that he could concentrate on the adventure at hand.

The sheer exuberance of *The Castle of Cagliostro* is infectious, but it is Miyazaki's command of the form that keeps it engaging even at such a breakneck pace. Key to this is the way he balances finely observed, realistic details with exaggerated movement and expression. All Miyazaki's films juggle internal realism with distorted embellishment and it is in the mix of the two that the films, and individual scenes within them, find their voice. *The Castle of Cagliostro* is skewed towards exaggeration because this matches the characters' larger-than-life personas and their roles in this gloriously pulpy story, but it still maintains some grounding in the real world. The barnstorming opening car chase, rumoured to be one of Steven Spielberg's favourites, is a case in point, a madcap and exciting sequence that sees Lupin and Jigen attempting to save Clarisse from being kidnapped by a group of hoodlums. As thrilling as anything from *The French Connection* (1971), the bending of real-world physics – the car driving along the mountainside at a clearly impossible angle – is tempered by focusing on utterly believable details, such as the way crumpled parts of Clarisse's increasingly battered 2CV fly through the air or the shattering of glass when Lupin punches out the windscreen. It makes the more outlandish elements appear fully congruous.

The Castle of Cagliostro excels in its numerous action scenes, creating a real sense of urgency. The rooftop scenes at the castle are dizzying, recalling similar sequences in Hitchcock's comedy *To Catch a Thief* (1955). Typical of Miyazaki is when the focus shifts to the interaction between man and machine as Jigen tries to control the Duke's autogyro while under fire from his henchmen. The vehicle is lovingly and accurately detailed, especially when careening out of control and knocking chunks from the castle roof. The climax – the extended duel between the Duke and Lupin – takes place inside a clock tower, which encapsulates the sense of scale, perspective and urgency set against the mechanical precision of the clock's deadly innards.

Also of interest is the way that Miyazaki focuses on his two main female characters. Clarisse appears to be no more than a damsel in distress but, despite her passivity, she does maintain some degree of plucky independence – trying to shield an unconscious Lupin from the tommy-gun spray of the Duke's creepy henchman. Ultimately she accepts the Duke's demand that she marry him in order to allow Lupin to go free. Far more striking is Lupin's ex-lover Fujiko, introduced as a mildly daring undercover reporter skulking around the castle, but who is eventually revealed as an action warrior, capable of rescuing Lupin from the jaws of death and holding Shadows at bay with a carefully lobbed grenade and a rat-a-tat of machine-gun fire.

The Castle of Cagliostro's reputation grew in the years following its release and it is held in high regard. When the then Emperor's daughter Princess Sayako was married in 2005 it was widely reported that her wedding dress was modelled on that of Clarisse. In a 2007 poll of favourite TV or movie anime conducted in Japan, *The Castle of Cagliostro* came in fifth. Miyazaki's debut feature film was a palpable hit.

Downtown Story (aka Chie the Brat) (Jarinko Chie) (1981)

Directed by: Takahata Isao

In downtown Ōsaka, feisty schoolgirl Chie serves sake and yakitori to the clients at her father Tetsu's small restaurant. Tetsu, meanwhile, gambles away any profits at the local *yakuza* house, his mighty fists, drinking and temper getting him into all sorts of trouble. Chie is left to mind the business alone, occasionally aided by the fiercely loyal cat Kotetsu. Kotetsu ruins the life of the local *yakuza* chief by ripping a testicle from his bruiser cat Antonio, the ensuing loss of masculine feline pride resulting in death by dog. Antonio's stuffed body now serves as a shrine in the reformed chief's new *okonomiyaki* (pancake/pizza) venture. Chie is desperately trying to balance all the elements of her life – school, the approaching marathon run, secret meetings with her mother (who has left Tetsu) and keeping her father from the cash she's stashed away. But matters come to a head when the son of Antonio seeks vengeance on Kotetsu.

Etsumi Haruki's successful manga, published in Futabasha's *Manga Action* magazine, followed the life of Chie as she copes with a family that has broken down, a difficult father and all the other problems experienced by any ten-year-old girl. The setting is crucial – Ōsaka, often described as Japan's second city whose people are renowned for their down-to-earth attitude and love of food. Equally important is the language used, Kansai-ben, a distinct dialect of the region. In both the film and the manga Chie's increasingly broad use of Kansai-ben indicates her level of anger, either when dealing with a cheating customer or preparing to deliver another weighty blow to her big-eared embarrassment of a father. By contrast, when speaking to her mother at their clandestine meetings, her language is far more polite and less abrasive. Takahata and Ōtsuka Yasuo spent some time ensuring the elements of downtown Ōsaka were accurate in the film – the eponymous Ōsaka Tower, Tsūtenkaku, is present in many background shots – as well as trying to piece together a narrative from the vignettes that make up Etsumi's manga. Despite the quality of the finished film, its production time was just a few months, resulting in the characters having a more solid style (suited to anime and easier to animate) than the sketched feel of the manga.

Although the film naturally gravitates towards Chie, its given English title *Downtown Story* is more appropriate than the more widely known title *Chie the Brat*, as this is a story about communities and how they interact. Chie herself, while capable of violent behaviour and inappropriate use of harsh language, is less a brat and more a resilient survivor with a game plan that looks towards re-establishing some kind of happy family life. All this coupled with the film's subtexts – marriage breakdown, deception, school difficulties, gangsters, gambling and alcoholism – make *Downtown Story* sound like a grim prospect but nothing could be further from the truth, as the film is played, for the most part, for laughs. As with many of Takahata's films, this makes the poignant moments all the more affecting.

The humour in *Downtown Story* is broad and occasionally bawdy with characters slugging it out like human versions of Tom and Jerry, their exaggerated expressions as another chair gets smashed over them priceless examples of the animator's art. This, then, is the comedy of dysfunction that would eventually feed into *My Neighbours the Yamadas* but *Downtown Story*, despite episodic sequences, manages to be a more rounded story. There are also hints of the testicular pride of the *tanuki* in *Pom Poko* as Kotetsu's battle with Antonio is slowly revealed to the viewer. Antonio, once proud, now dead and stuffed, has a set of crossed sticking plasters marking where his right testicle had once been. Further examples of this bawdy humour originate from Chie's father Tetsu (she finds it difficult calling him 'Dad') whose lack of social skills and shame are borderline frightening. Ever out for a quick yen, he makes a bet that the next person walking past will be a boy. When it turns out to be Chie he declares that she is a boy and should show her naughty bits to prove it. Needless to say, Chie gives him a round beating. Despite all this, however, there is a hint of redemption not only in Tetsu but everyone in the film. Food plays a vital role in that it seems to be a signifier of reconciliation, albeit coupled with the damning excesses of sake. Chie manages a restaurant and is successful. Following the demise of Antonio, the *yakuza* chief turns his back on gambling and opens an *okonomiyaki* restaurant instead, achieving salvation even if his snot-enhanced seafood special is a touch salty. Similarly, the gangsters who try and intimidate the reformed chief eventually turn from crime to become the

Caramel Brothers, selling their sweet confectionery at the local fair.

Downtown Story is hilarious and occasionally moving – a raucous comedy with empathetic characters. In particular, the anthropomorphic cats (they speak in such a way that we can understand them but the human characters can't) provide both relief and conflict, acting out a feline microcosm of the world at large with karate showdowns and spaghetti-western mannerisms. Certain kinds of humour can be difficult to translate, which probably explains why *Downtown Story* has not received the kind of distribution outside of Japan that one would expect for a film by such a famous director. This is a pity as beneath the comic violence lies a film with a real heart. *Downtown Story* was modestly successful across Japan but proved immensely popular in the Kansai region and spawned a television series that continued the (mis)adventures of Chie and her problematic family and community. Takahata was involved with a number of the earlier episodes in this 64-part series but eventually drifted away from the project.

Gōshu the Cellist (Sero Hiki no Gōshu) (1982)

Directed by: Takahata Isao

Gōshu is a cellist in an orchestra that provides musical accompaniment to popular films at the local cinema. The musicians, and particularly the grumpy conductor, have grander plans for their musical talents and are seeking to win a prestigious competition. The only fly in their ointment is young Gōshu, whose playing is distinctly mediocre. Frustrated, Gōshu practises his cello diligently every night, but is interrupted by a variety of animals: a cat who has the audacity to give him one of his own tomatoes, a critical cuckoo, a rhythmic raccoon and a maudlin mouse who claims that the cello music is needed to cure her sick child. Although he is annoyed by these disruptions, they nevertheless push his playing to new heights.

Although television work was always available, Miyazaki and Takahata wanted to work on personal films, but this proved to be a difficult venture. *Gōshu the Cellist* (*Sero Hiki no Gōshu* – literally 'Gōshu's Cello Playing') was no exception; it took Takahata six years to bring it to the screen. The company that finally bankrolled the picture, Oh! Productions, had primarily provided animation services for other people's films, including *A Dog of Flanders*, *The Castle of Cagliostro* and *Conan, the Boy in Future*, but this was the first production that they backed themselves. Takahata's attraction to the story was clear – Miyazawa Kenji's elegant children's tale was ideal for conversion to the animated form, filled with rich music and anthropomorphised animals. Despite the apparent simplicity of the story there are a number of complex cultural, environmental and moral themes running through the film. Miyazawa is probably best remembered for his children's stories and poetry but he was also an agriculturalist who strived to improve the lives of farmers through practical application such as the introduction of more efficient farming methods and seed varieties. These links to the land, of environmental empathy through human art, can be seen in the interactions between the human Gōshu and the animal world, which start off as antagonistic and end up as mutually beneficial. Like his most famous protagonist, Miyazawa was also a cellist and his cello is now on display at a museum dedicated to his legacy of art, chemistry, writing and music in the city of Hanamaki in northern Japan.

The links between music and cinema are particularly strong in Japan where film language developed a notably different aesthetic from the classical Hollywood model. Japan continued to show silent film – or rather film accompanied by music and narration, the latter performed by *benshi* who were often more famous than the stars of the film – after most other countries had adopted synchronised sound. Gōshu's job with a cinema orchestra reinforces these connections, but we see that he also aspires to finding higher employment in more respected venues, such as concert halls. Rather than viewing this as a bourgeois aspiration, both the film and Miyazawa's text see the benefits of group working and collective experience – Gōshu's improved playing doesn't just widen his own horizons; it also makes life better for the orchestra and audience. Takahata's film reinforces this process by employing long passages of classical music – especially Beethoven – to illustrate Gōshu's progress. Integrating classical music with animation is not a new concept, Disney's *Silly Symphonies* (1929-39) and the experimental *Fantasia* all embraced the idea, but here music is important to the meaning of the film. Music is Gōshu's occupation but is also seen as necessary to spiritual well-being, literally in the case of the animals who huddle around Gōshu's little cabin seeking an aural cure for their ailments, but also in the joy of the cinema and concert audiences. Gōshu's choice of practice pieces also reflects his frustrations and eventually a burgeoning understanding of his relationship with his environment. When the first creature comes to visit, Gōshu becomes irate and cruel, chastising the cat for stealing his tomato and torturing the poor creature by playing the piece 'Tiger Hunt in India' at such a pace that the cat ricochets off the walls in agony. Although he eventually realises the benefits that the animals have given his playing, he still approaches life with sceptical caution – he erroneously believes that the request for an encore is perhaps a form of joke, so he plays 'Tiger Hunt in India' with the aim of similarly affecting the audience. But his unorthodox training means that he is now a virtuoso cellist, and the agonised responses of the cat have now been transformed into rapturous applause.

The animation in *Gōshu the Cellist* is deceptively simple; the film is set in a few modest locations with the key encounters usually limited to a couple of on-screen characters. As with Japanese brush paintings, it is the elegance and simplicity that conveys the true essence of a subject, unencumbered by superfluous showmanship and unnecessary ostentation. Further evidence of this uncluttered approach to the film can be seen in Takahata's animatics for the production, which are light and breezy but totally expressive, often indicating meaning with just a handful of pencil strokes. The character designs and the closely observed movements of the animals are carefully realised. This is balanced against the anthropomorphised characteristics of the animals – the cat's utterly realistic walking outside Gōshu's house contrasts with an almost Chuck Jones-style manic exaggeration of movement when subjected to 'Tiger Hunt in India'. Similarly, the raccoon-dog becomes more obviously animated when purposefully rolling out a sheet of music or drumming on Gōshu's cello. This anthropomorphic creature provides the basis for the raccoon-dogs (*tanuki*) in *Pom Poko*, where the extremes of animation's ability to reflect real life *and* depict exaggerated absurdity are explored in vivid detail.

Although *Gōshu the Cellist* had been filmed a number of times prior to Takahata's version, including one production that used puppets, his remains the best-loved of the adaptations, a truly delightful and delicate film that is both moving and uplifting. Studio Ghibli also set about adapting a story by Miyazawa Kenji in the shape of *The Night of Taneyamagahara* (2006), a short film released on DVD to coincide with the 110th anniversary of the author's birth.

Nausicaä of the Valley of the Wind (Kaze no tani no Naushika) (1984)

Directed by: Miyazaki Hayao
Produced by: Takahata Isao

> *'1,000 years have passed since Earth succumbed to pollution generated by the very nations we now inhabit. Most of Earth is covered by the highly toxic Sea of Corruption.'*

The Seven Days of Fire, when the Warrior Giants decimated the Earth, has left a long and terrifying legacy. One thousand years on, Earth is an uninhabitable wasteland of filth, a toxic miasma that can kill humans unless they wear protective masks. Isolated communities have sprung up in the pockets of land that can still sustain life, on the boundaries of forests or in the valleys, but the Sea of Corruption is spreading, so the Earth's remaining tribes need to be extra vigilant if they are to avoid the spread of deadly spores. The tribe of the Valley of the Wind are one such group, trying to live a sustainable life.

Nausicaä is the daughter of the Valley of the Wind's King Jhil and an enthusiastic adventurer, studying the flora and fauna that lie beyond her village, outside in the toxic zone. Most fascinating of all the creatures are the Ohmu, huge insects that shed their armoured shells as they grow, leaving exoskeletons that are harder than ceramic. Nausicaä's flying skills are prodigious but even she is powerless to prevent a Tolmekian warship from crashing into the mountainside by her peaceful village. The only survivor, the shackled Lastelle of Pejite, croaks a dire warning about the contents of the warship. Lastelle is all too right for it contains the body of one of the Warrior Giants, and, before long, Princess Kushana of the Tolmekian storms into the Valley of the Wind in order to realise her plan to raise the ancient god to life and conquer the toxic zone. She removes all threats by attacking tribes who get in her way, a fate the Valley of the Wind now faces, made all too clear when her troops murder Jhil. Nausicaä is taken hostage by the Tolmekians to keep her village in line, but she escapes and, joined by Lastelle's brother Asbel and the feisty squirrel-fox Teto, discovers a fertile land that exists beneath the world's surface. Armed with this knowledge, she needs to get home and somehow convince Kushana not to revive the Warrior Giant. But matters become more urgent when a stampede of irate Ohmu, infuriated at the torture of their young, descend upon the Valley of the Wind, hell-bent on revenge.

Nausicaä was so important in the creation of Studio Ghibli that it is often mistakenly thought of as a Ghibli film, and has subsequently been released under that very label. But *Nausicaä*'s inception and the audience reaction to it are far more complex, and the film's commercial success was a surprise for a production that was limited in budget and tight on schedule. In a way, *Nausicaä* was never meant to be a film. It started life on the pages of Tokuma Shoten Publishing's *Animage* magazine, a publication dedicated primarily to examining the anime market. Miyazaki had been persuaded to provide a manga for the magazine, but he did so on the condition that he had complete control over his script and that the work would be on an ad hoc basis. When beginning *Nausicaä*, Miyazaki was finding it difficult to get regular animation work, so his contributions were frequent. Paradoxically, this delayed the manga as a regular feature because its success led to negotiations for making a film of the story. Miyazaki would eventually finish the tale over 12 years later with episodes appearing sporadically. It is ironic that Miyazaki had used the epic and detailed manga to represent a Moebius-style landscape that would be inherently difficult to animate. The parent company of *Animage* agreed to bankroll the project as a feature-length film, employing animators on a 'per cel' basis – i.e. they would be paid for each cel they produced rather than being on contract – to keep down costs, leaving much of the coordination to Miyazaki and a reluctant Takahata, who was drafted in to produce the film. The production ran at a breakneck pace with barely ten months between its inception and release – astonishing for such an ambitious film. It was necessary to cut down on some of the details but ultimately this meant that the film hones in on important points and does allow time for some truly spectacular sequences. When it was released in the cinema *Nausicaä* took Japan by storm and remains, for many, one of Miyazaki's most admired films. It's easy to see why, for, to all intents and purposes, this is a quintessentially Ghibli film bursting with the themes and ideas that would feed into Miyazaki's future projects. The film's predominant theme is that of environmentalism and of humankind's relationship with the Earth.

A thousand years of misery are the result of mankind's pollution. Mirroring this is the rift between the film's two central female characters, Nausicaä (whose name may well have come from the princess of the Phaeacians in Homer's *Odyssey*) and Kushana. On the surface this is very simple – Kushana is the evil, tyrannical dictator while Nausicaä is the benevolent champion of her people – but this is too simplistic. Ultimately the two royals' proposed aim is the same: to rid the world of toxicity. Their methods are what separates them. Nausicaä seeks an answer through study, through knowing her environment and being part of it. She empathises with the creatures that roam the wastelands, scuttling through the skeletal remains of civilisations lost. Kushana's solution is through obliteration of the toxicity and all that represents it; the insects that have attacked her body have left her half-robotic and full of malice. For her, the ends, however terrible, justify the means. Conflict versus harmony: technology versus nature. Nausicaä is another in the long line of strong female characters in Miyazaki's films. She is spirited, reverential and full of vigour and, although royalty, has a genuine concern for her subjects.

The influence of *Nausicaä of the Valley of the Wind* on future productions is profound: the communities of *Princess Mononoke*, the environmental respect of *My Neighbour Totoro*, the powerful gods of *Spirited Away*. Miyazaki Gorō's *Tales from Earthsea* owes a huge debt to this film, even down to the tapestry-style opening credits and the crumbling bridges. But *Nausicaä* also has its roots in other Miyazaki projects, notably in a manga he was drawing at the time of its conception, *The Journey of Shuna* (*Shuna no tabi*, 1983), a beautiful, watercolour story with strikingly similar designs. The feel of the film and its art also recalls the work of Moebius (Jean Giraud), the French science-fiction comic artist with whom Miyazaki would later have a joint exhibition of art in Paris. Miyazaki and Moebius had also been briefly involved in the long gestation of *Little Nemo*, from the stories of the father of traditional animation Winsor McCay.

Nausicaä of the Valley of the Wind marks the first collaboration between Miyazaki and composer Joe Hisaishi (Mamoru Fujisawa), who was persuaded to work on the film soon after its inception. Hisaishi was keen to use his skills as an electronic-music experimenter with an interest in minimalist music to give the film a distinctive, otherworldly feel that was half-rhythmic and half-familiar composition – primitive music from 1,000 years in the future. The two men became friends and Hisaishi has created the soundtracks for all Miyazaki's subsequent feature films, moving away from electronica and into more orchestral scores.

Although *Nausicaä of the Valley of the Wind* was an unqualified success commercially and critically, it also marked the start of an occasionally strained relationship between Miyazaki and those who distribute his films outside Japan, particularly in the USA. This would result in US distributors trying to cut, of all things, *My Neighbour Totoro* as well as trying to tone down the violent content of *Princess Mononoke*, something they failed to do because Miyazaki rightly held fast to the principle that his work should be distributed without alteration. It was a lesson he learned the hard way – *Nausicaä of the Valley of the Wind* was released in the US a year after its Japanese debut in a poorly dubbed print that had over 20 minutes of footage removed. It destroyed the environmental message, confused the plot and changed the characters' names (Nausicaä became Zandra for some inexplicable reason). The result – *Warriors of the Wind* – is still watchable but a mangled mess compared with its source.

Nausicaä of the Valley of the Wind gave Miyazaki and Takahata the confidence and impetus to create their own animations their own way, directly leading to the formation of Studio Ghibli.

THE FILMS OF STUDIO GHIBLI

Laputa: Castle in the Sky (Tenkū no shiro Rapyuta) (1986)

Written and directed by: Miyazaki Hayao

> *'Many people of my generation see the miners as a symbol;*
> *a dying breed of fighting men. Now they are gone.' Miyazaki*
> *Hayao, Guardian*, 14 September 2005

> *'The word, which I interpret the flying or floating island, is*
> *in the original Laputa, whereof I could never learn the true*
> *etymology.' Gulliver's Travels*

Pazu, an enthusiastic and dedicated worker in a remote mining village, finds that his life changes for ever when he catches the body of a girl who falls slowly from the sky into his arms. She is Sheeta, recently ejected from the ship of dapper cad Muska who has kidnapped her as part of a reprehensible scheme to reclaim the power of the fabled Laputa. Sheeta holds the key to finding the legendary flying island. Pazu, too, harbours a desire to see the floating lands that his late father claimed once to have glimpsed, though the only evidence of this is a fading sepia photograph of a land shrouded in cloud. Less idealistic in their motives are the Dola Clan, a ruthless band of misfit pirates led by the cackling Mama Dola, always guaranteed to cause maximum mayhem in the pursuit of plunder. When Sheeta is once again captured by

Muska, Pazu must form an uneasy alliance with the Dola Clan in order to rescue her. But Muska's plans are more insidious than anyone could have imagined. He has obtained one of the robots from the flying land of Laputa and seeks to resuscitate it, using its terrible might to subjugate the world, a plan he hopes will be achieved by harnessing the power of the floating island. The only way his evil plans can be halted is through the intervention of a determined boy and a disparate clan of scallywags.

In 1984, Miyazaki visited Wales at a defining moment in the UK's power struggle between workers, employers and the state. The miners' strike was in full swing. Margaret Thatcher's government sought the closure of pits deemed unprofitable and the result was mass unemployment. Affected by his experiences Miyazaki returned to the country two years later to research *Laputa*, by which time the union movement had been crushed. This is not, however, a sledgehammer look at an industry in decline of the sort portrayed in domestic films like *Billy Elliot* (2000) or *Brassed Off* (1996) or reflected in the live-action Japanese film *Hula Girls* (2006). Rather, it uses the milieu as a background for a story of solid, meaningful, community toil set against a gripping tale of fantasy and adventure. Although never explicitly stated in the film, Pazu's community is effectively an alternate late-nineteenth-century Wales. Welsh mining provides the setting for the film but there are other visual influences, some of the establishing shots recalling the work of LS Lowry in their misty angular industrialisation.

Laputa: Castle in the Sky was the first film from the newly formed Studio Ghibli. Having taken the profits from the hugely successful *Nausicaä of the Valley of the Wind* and raised further funding from Tokuma Shoten, Takahata and Miyazaki formed the company in order to produce animation free from outside interference and with strong rights for its personnel. The formation of Ghibli had some degree of uncertainty attached to it because of the nature of the projects the studio wanted to produce. These were personal films with no guarantee of public acceptance. From a marketing point of view, *Laputa: Castle in the Sky* contained enough elements to pre-sell it; it had adventure and humour, and science fiction was a popular genre. However, the choice of a European mining town as a setting, and the trappings of anachronistic flying machines and environmental mysticism made it a harder sell.

Laputa, the floating island, can be raised and lowered in Jonathan Swift's *Gulliver's Travels* using magnetism, but Miyazaki's island is powered by crystals. Indeed, Pazu rejects the fictional country by noting, 'There's a Laputa in Swift's *Gulliver's Travels*, but that was made up.' Miyazaki's love of flying and tactile flying devices pervades the film. Pazu dreams of flying to Laputa, Muska commands a huge dirigible and the pirates own a flying craft from which they launch their 'flaptors' – buzzing, wasp-like contraptions that dash over the landscape with insect precision. Flying represents freedom and power – Sheeta's magic pendant enables her to float in the sky and Pazu's doves are released to the winds when he realises that he may not return to his village. It gives Miyazaki the opportunity to construct his world unrestricted by ground and gravity. A case in point is the joyous scene of Pazu in the 'flaptor', the ground whizzing by below him in a breathtaking blur.

The blending of mysticism and mechanism is what makes *Laputa: Castle in the Sky* more science fantasy than science fiction, its alternate universe familiar but different, recalling the feel of French comic *Métal Hurlant* in its more lyrical moments. Laputa's source of power comes from the black mineral that contains mystical powers but dims when exposed, the exception being Sheeta's stone, which retains its magical state.

But this mythical mineral is exploited, just as the mines in Pazu's community are exploited for their tin and silver. It is used to control mechanical devices, chief among which are the huge, lopsided robots who tend the lands long after their masters have ceased to be. We are first introduced to these creatures when Muska revives one. As it lurches into life, its exposed wires writhing eagerly in the expectation of being connected once more, this metal Titan eradicates an army of men, spewing out laser death from its emotionless face and dissecting buildings with a sweep of its head. For Muska this is just a prelude to the 'heavenly power that destroyed Sodom and Gomorrah' that he later unleashes on Laputa itself, scattering soldiers from the floating rock like the doomed passengers of Winsor McCay's *The Sinking of the Lusitania* (1918). As an heir to the Laputan throne, Muska (aka Romska Palo Ul Laputa) sees his role as harnessing the power he perceives his ancestors had and using it to command – 'Their dread power to rule the Earth.' But Sheeta (aka Lusheeta Toel Ul Laputa) is also an heir and reveals that this may not be the way forward, demanding that the robots halt their destruction. When she and Pazu arrive on Laputa they see one of the robots in action after years of solitude, tending its master's grave with a carefully picked flower. Technology and machinery are not intrinsically bad; it is human application that makes them deadly.

One of the film's chief delights is the way in which Miyazaki subverts our expectations and prejudices of what we expect to see in a genre film. The giant robots are a good example. We expect a giant robot in a film to go crazy and destroy things, but Miyazaki also shows us its tender side, confounding our initial impressions. Similarly, the women's roles in Miyazaki's films often deviate from gender stereotypes, his female characters showing strong convictions and determination – from the frying-pan-wielding mother in Pazu's village to the complex figure of Mama Dola. Dola is one of Miyazaki's finest characters. In most films the elderly are defined by infirmity and nostalgia or are often absent altogether, but Miyazaki's films, while often featuring youthful protagonists, acknowledge the elderly as part of the community. Dola, however, is an old lady like no other; the ruthless but ultimately redeemable leader of a pirate gang, she is animated, irascible and thoroughly disreputable, her mockingly girlish pigtails offset by her rotten-toothed grin and impish cackling. No quiet bus rides to the supermarket for this violent, larcenous pensioner, although she absolves herself by maintaining a sense of community with her gang and ultimately doing the right thing, even if it is for her own gain. Not so Muska, whose similar motivation of greed is defined by self-interest and megalomania.

Laputa: Castle in the Sky's strong story, its sense of adventure and its wealth of memorable characters have made it one of Miyazaki's most popular films, particularly outside of Japan. Fortunately, the film was a critical success, topping a number of polls for best film and ensuring that Studio Ghibli became a credible organisation. However, the film's financial returns were modest, meaning that they needed to seek additional funding for future projects.

The Story of the Yanagawa Canals (1987)

Directed by: Takahata Isao

> *'If we give up our water, we'll never get it back.'*

The Story of the Yanagawa Canals offers a look at the remarkable canals of the town of Yanagawa, a centuries-old fixture on the landscape that served the community for many years like life-giving veins running between their houses. Following the increase in Japan's economic growth in the 1960s these canals became clogged with sludge, forming stagnant breeding grounds for mosquitoes and disease as the population rejected traditional ways of living and turned to consumer goods and thoughtless disposal. The canals were slowly replaced with concrete and plastic piping. It was a situation that occurred in other Japanese towns as well, but in Yanagawa the community fought back, struggling to regain their canals and restore them to their former glory under the championing of campaigner Hiromatsu. This film tells the story of the canals' history, Yanagawa's restoration, the science behind it and the effect of the revitalised canals on a new generation.

Flushed with the success of *Nausicaä*, Miyazaki set about looking for other projects to film and, following a visit to Yanagawa, thought the locale might provide a tranquil backdrop to a new animated tale. It was suggested that Takahata might be interested in the project but, on visiting the town, he became fascinated by the true story behind the incredible canal system and the work of the local population to keep it running. The animated story was dropped – although there are some Miyazaki-helmed animated sequences in the film depicting how canal life worked in the past – and instead Takahata spent a number of years on and off filming a live-action documentary. Clearly this was unlikely to be a commercially lucrative project so *The Story of the Yanagawa Canals* was bankrolled by Miyazaki, who became executive producer on the film. Thus, despite being filmed after the formation of Ghibli and despite its release under the Ghibli banner, it isn't strictly a Ghibli film, but more a personally funded project. It does, however, touch on many of the themes that are familiar from the animated films of Takahata.

The Story of the Yanagawa Canals is a fascinating documentary about our relationship with nature, the effect of the economic boom on post-war Japan and the power of genuine community spirit. It is a meticulous film about the history and techniques of canal maintenance and the community responsible for that maintenance – an exhaustive, and, at nearly three hours long, sometimes exhausting dissection of a town and its people. In many ways this is one of Takahata's most life-affirming and positive films, harking back to the social spirit of his debut *Horusu* in that the outcome for the characters is not only hard won but just and worthwhile. *The Story of the Yanagawa Canals* also portrays that rare beast, the decent politician. Hiromatsu's insight into his town's needs makes him the hero of the piece – holding public meetings and persuading the mayor to adopt his radical, traditional ideas. But ultimately it is the community that are the real saviours of their homes, banding together, regardless of social status, and doing the hard graft necessary to return the canals to their former glory. As in the flashback scenes in *Pom Poko*, Takahata is not so idealistic as to assume that mankind doesn't have an effect on the environment, but he does show how there can be a sustainable compromise. It is refreshing to see the mantra 'Living with nature, disposing of waste by recycling' being applied successfully – the townsfolk may have to work hard, but they are rewarded ultimately by a cleaner environment, a decline in mosquitoes and the removal of the stench of sewage and stagnation.

The use of traditional ways of washing, recycling and maintenance may seem like a coy return to some rural Luddite idyll, but Takahata shows how these traditions can sit beside modern conveniences when things are properly thought through. Links to Japan's roots are shown by focusing on environmental Shintō moat-drying parties with their decorative floats and appetising carp sushi as well as through the legends of *kappa* (water *yōkai* that children are warned will take them away if they urinate in the river). This link to the past is also evident in the celebratory Okinohata festival, run entirely by and for the people, featuring a float parade and made possible through the tireless efforts of performers, organisers and caterers. Takahata's affinity with Japanese poetry is also an important part of this film, and he relates the area to its most famous poet Kitahara Hakushū, a prolific writer and one of the twentieth century's most important Japanese poets.

Although unlikely to appeal to the broader audience for Ghibli's animated films, *The Story of the Yanagawa Canals* is nevertheless an interesting work because it focuses on many of the themes that pepper Takahata's anime. Visually, his use of relational editing and slow tracking shots recalls the similar style of his more controlled works, but, despite being a very low-key and personal film, it is one that celebrates the wider spirit of community.

Grave of the Fireflies (Hotaru no haka) **(1988)**

Written (screenplay) and directed by: Takahata Isao

'Why do fireflies have to die so soon?'

In the closing months of World War Two, Japan is suffering from the relentless assault of Allied bombs, which is razing its cities with ceaseless, dispassionate destruction. Kōbe is no different and fearful families take to meagre air-raid shelters when the sirens announce a further burst of fiery devastation. Teenager Seita and his younger sister Setsuko survive the latest attack to rain molten death on the city. Their mother, however, is caught in the firestorm and her bloodied, bandaged body sustains such extensive burns that she dies in front of Seita. He decides to hide the news from Setsuko, saying that they will see her again when she recovers from a slight illness. In order to survive, Seita recovers some of the family possessions that were deliberately buried for just such an emergency and eventually seeks shelter with his aunt who lives in Nishinomiya. But his refusal to take an active part in the household's duties leads to a fracas with his aunt and he takes off with Setsuko, finding a new home in a disused air-raid shelter. The pair survive on stolen food and grilled frogs but Setsuko is beginning to show the tell-tale signs of malnourishment.

Studio Ghibli still required external funding to realise their more personal projects. Publishers Shinchosha wanted to film the award-winning book *Grave of the Fireflies* and were keen to have Ghibli involved. Takahata agreed to take on the film when they negotiated a deal to part-finance not only *Grave of the Fireflies*, but also Miyazaki's personal project *My Neighbour Totoro*. Miyazaki's whimsical masterpiece appeared on the surface to be a childish distraction while *Grave of the Fireflies* was a harrowing account of Japan's final devastating year as a participant in World War Two. In order to give both titles the best chance the films were released as a double bill – probably the most emotionally devastating three hours ever devised. The double bill did not set the box office alight – initially. *Totoro* would eventually become the mascot for Studio Ghibli, shifting a bewildering number of merchandise spin-offs, a trade that, over 30 years on, shows no sign of slowing down. *Grave of the Fireflies*, meanwhile, became Ghibli's calling card to the world, generating much critical acclaim and raising the international profile of the fledgling studio.

Based upon the Naoki Prize-winning 1967 story by Nosaka Akiyuki, a semi-autobiographical work written by the author to exorcise his own wartime demons and guilt over the death of his sister, *Grave of the Fireflies* is a tightly focused film that centres primarily on two characters, Seita and Setsuko. The Allied bombings of Japan were intense, relentless and devastating, creating firestorms that engulfed traditional Japanese wooden and paper homes. Although the bombing of Tōkyō and the nuclear bombs dropped on Nagasaki and Hiroshima are most famously recalled, the plethora of other cities razed to the ground is less documented. *Grave of the Fireflies* is not a war film in the traditional sense but rather a film about the consequences of war and its effect on individuals, away from the headline-grabbing big battles and army manoeuvres. This small but poignant subgenre of autobiographical outpourings has occasionally surfaced in anime from the stark horror of Nakazawa Keiji's *Barefoot Gen* (1983), about the author trying to stay alive in Hiroshima after the atom bomb, to *Rail of the Star* (1997). Takahata's astonishing film has power and intensity partly due to its claustrophobic focus but also because this is a very human story populated by believable and flawed characters. It is uncomfortable to watch not just because of the characters' extraordinary circumstances but because their misguided decisions are all too real.

A key element that marks out *Grave of the Fireflies* is that its main protagonist is not a hero in the traditional sense. Seita is intent on ensuring his sister's survival and is fiercely protective of her, but ultimately he is proud, pig-headed, reactionary and irresponsible. Although we can identify with his emotions and predicament we cannot agree with his decisions and actions, or rather inaction. This is plain from the very opening of the film – Seita's pathetic and anonymous death in a station subway, his head drooping one final time as the light in his eyes is extinguished and the flies gather around his wasted corpse. 'Another one,' bemoans the station cleaner as we see that Seita is not the only person who has died that night, 21 September 1945, a month after Japan had surrendered. The film's narration is, like *Sunset Boulevard* (1950), a post-mortem from Seita's spirit's point of view, his pitiful last breaths serving as a comment on how he chose to live his life. Had he decided to stay with his aunt and swallow his pride, both he and his precious sister would still be alive. Likewise, if he'd decided to look for work he may not have died a lonely, remorseful death. The fact that he is so focused on his own and his sister's survival rather than on his community and wider family is ultimately what kills him – individualism in a time of crisis is shown as a bad thing. His bitter aunt becomes increasingly demanding and sells his mother's kimono in order to buy rice, ultimately leading to altercations and the siblings' departure from the household. Rather than sorting out a long-term solution to his problems, or apologising to his aunt, he steals food at a time when rationing is in place. He even resorts to breaking into people's houses during air raids and is constantly castigated by the community for his attitude – 'Don't you know there's a war going on...?' But while it is easy to criticise his decisions from an adult perspective, it must be remembered that Seita is a child, desperately trying to do the best for his sister, however misguided.

Grave of the Fireflies shows us a microcosm of the effects of war and the way that conflict can dehumanise people. This is not a film about soldiers – only passing mention is made of Seita's father's naval career – but about civilians who have little understanding of the nature or purpose of war. It demonstrates how the horror of conflict and exposure to atrocity can desensitise and destroy human emotion, indeed humanity itself. This is clear from the exasperated but resigned remarks made by the cleaner about the way in which Seita's mother is treated. After she is fatally injured in the firestorm, doctors working at a local school do everything in their power to keep her alive, to no avail. Once she has painfully passed on, matters become callously practical – her maggot-ridden body is dumped on a funeral pyre along with the other victims, her ashes indistinguishable from those who died with her. As he becomes increasingly malnourished Seita struggles to hold on to any humanity, his soul surviving only by channelling his emotions through his sister. When she is finally gone his remorse is palpable, and, knowing he has effectively killed his sibling, he drifts into despondency and death.

Fireflies serve a number of purposes in the film, both as plot device and metaphor. Fireflies provide the last fleeting glimpses of happiness when the siblings go on a hunt after seeing planes pass over them – a return to healthier times when the pair used to catch the bugs, Setsuko learning the fragility of life when she accidentally squishes one in her hands. Indeed, it is the very fleeting nature of the firefly that makes it such a poignant symbol – a short, fragile life that burns brightly but fades, like Setsuko herself, optimistic and lively but doomed to an early grave. Fireflies also represent the aeroplanes, little buzzing lights in the sky – only their scale and distance differentiate them from the insects. And then there are the bombs that rain down, causing flowers of flame to burn bright and deadly. On a more microcosmic level, the fireflies' grave outside the pair's air-raid-shelter home is marked by the empty tin of Sakuma Drops, the hard-boiled fruit sweets that Setsuko enjoys so much. The tin eventually becomes the vessel for her ashes. Takahata commented, 'To live is everything. In turning *Grave of the Fireflies* into animated form I wanted to show the audience how these two siblings lived.'

Grave of the Fireflies is a universal film about the consequences of war and a devastating emotional experience.

My Neighbour Totoro (Tonari no Totoro) (1988)

Written and directed by: Miyazaki Hayao

Satsuki and her younger sister Mei move with their father to an old country house so that they can be close to the hospital where their sick mother is convalescing. In comparison with city living the house seems huge, and the girls are delighted at the prospect that the place might be haunted. *Sugoi!* And this certainly appears to be the case, dust bunnies scuttling away whenever light enters a room and acorns appearing in unlikely places. One day an adventurous Mei comes across a strange creature and decides to follow it but, realising it is being tailed, the snowy white animal vanishes. Undeterred, Mei follows another of the creatures, a young Totoro carrying a bag of acorns, through a corridor of undergrowth that makes a passage under the shadow of the huge camphor tree that dominates the forest skyline. There, resting on his back, is towering Totoro, snoring. He slowly wakes when he realises that an excited Mei is perched upon his chest. After convincing her sister of the truth of this strange encounter, the pair pay their respects at the forest shrine and later spy the ocarina-playing Totoro balancing on the branch of a tree. This heralds the start of their adventures with the spirits of the forests.

Quite simply one of the most charming and magical films ever created, *My Neighbour Totoro*, amazingly, had great difficulties getting beyond the planning stage. At the time, Ghibli was not self-sufficient and needed investment to continue making films, so the studio sought backing from several sources. When the idea for *Totoro* was pitched, the potential backers pulled away from the project – it was too childish and there was no real conflict or action – who would want to see it? *Totoro* was finally given the green light when Takahata agreed to make *Grave of the Fireflies*. The financers hedged their bets on two products: a risky one that they wanted to make and Miyazaki's 'little kids' film', figuring they might make some sort of a return if just one of the two proved popular. Thus the most emotionally perplexing double bill of all time was conceived; at nearly three hours of heartache and joy there wouldn't be a dry eye in the house. Takahata noted, 'Those who saw *Totoro* first didn't want to see *Fireflies* to the end. Those who saw *Fireflies* first didn't have that problem, and stayed to the end. The double featuring was a problem.' *Grave of the Fireflies* went on to great international critical acclaim while Miyazaki's cherished project initially seemed destined for video and afternoon TV. But, once out in the open, *My Neighbour Totoro* didn't sink into bargain-bin oblivion but grew, like Mei and Satsuki's seeds, and Ghibli blossomed into a healthy, sustainable studio as the tale became ingrained in the national consciousness. Everyone wanted their own Totoro and finally Ghibli acquiesced to demands that they release a range of merchandise based upon the film. Until then, Ghibli had only licensed a small number of tie-in products for their films, preferring the work to stand on its own, but *Totoro* showed that, providing they had the right partners and complete control over what products were released, this could provide a lucrative sideline, helping finance future projects. Ghibli still tightly control product licences and there is a bewildering range of Totoro products – from cuddly toys of all the various characters and creatures, mobile-phone straps, calendars, clocks, watches, ocarinas, ties, playing cards, zippos and stationery.

So why is this gentle film so affecting? Primarily it is for two reasons: naturalism and wonder. The way the film has a complete affinity with the natural world, the way that believable characters interact with nature marks the film as light years away from, say, *ET: The Extra Terrestrial* (1982), which was, at the time, Japan's biggest box-office success and a film often compared with *Totoro*. Mei, Satsuki and even the boy next door, Kanta, are all believable characters far removed from the cloying, 'goody-two-shoes' protagonists that so often saturate the youth-film market. When we first meet the girls, they attempt to hide from a cyclist until they realise that, no, he isn't a policeman. They are good girls, helping with chores and enjoying a loving family life. It is the little details of their day-to-day living – bathing as a family, Satsuki's delight when her mother brushes her hair – that make the film so real. The detail in nature too – Mei watching tadpoles, the rustling of the trees – grounds the film in reality, albeit a nostalgic, rural one. The appearance of woodland spirits in this environment creates a sense of wonder but appears completely natural, as indeed it should, for the spirits aren't supernatural or extraterrestrial. Even though there is a sense that Mei and Satsuki can see Totoro because they are children, there is also an implication that they can only see him because they have an affinity and respect for the natural order of things. They bow to the sacred tree – 'Trees and people used to be good friends' – and show no fear of the spirit world, quite the opposite. By accepting this, the audience is drawn into a world that remains unseen to our cynical eyes outside of the cinema. *My Neighbour Totoro* is not just a children's film, but one that allows an adult audience to see once more through the eyes of a child. Miyazaki draws us into this world by slowly opening our eyes, escalating the revelations of the fantastical after a gradual introduction. First we have the *susuwatari*, or dust bunnies, jet-black balls of dust with inquisitive but nervous eyes, lurking in the corners of disused houses until the new owners release them into the forest. Then we meet smaller totoros before encountering Totoro himself. Totoro is a huge, furry, grey creature with an infectious grin. Despite the friendship that grows between Totoro and the girls he is not a figure to be taken lightly, his initial curiosity towards Mei only blossoming into a friendship when he realises that she is respectful. His mighty roar and magical powers mean that, while he is an admirable ally, he could also be a formidable foe. But therein lies the film's beauty, the lure of nature that can at once be beautiful and terrifying.

My Neighbour Totoro's boundless inventiveness soars even further with the entrance of a *nekobasu* (cat bus), a smiling, multi-limbed cat with headlight eyes that bounds frantically across the land. Passengers climb aboard via a door that magically appears in his side. The girls first come across this scampering transport when waiting for their father at a bus stop in the rain. Totoro joins them and the girls give him their umbrella when his leaf-based brolly proves somewhat ineffectual. The film's iconic moment is this dialogue-free scene of the three waiting in the downpour. Totoro's ride arrives first and the girls watch in astonishment as he boards the frenetic *nekobasu*. Later, in one of the film's many exhilarating scenes of flying, they get a ride themselves as Totoro arranges for a *nekobasu* to take the pair to see their mother, from afar, to check that she is alright. Miyazaki conveys all these relationships through image and movement; Totoro doesn't speak the same language as Mei and Satsuki, their communication occurring entirely through natural bonds.

My Neighbour Totoro, Miyazaki's small, personal (many have commented on the similarities with his own childhood when his mother was sick) film has become a national institution. Totoro quickly became the *de facto* mascot for Studio Ghibli, his imposing-but-benign profile preceding all the studio's films, with a smaller Totoro acting as a logo for the company that is both simple and full of character. Mei, striding confidently to camera, launches a slew of promotions for the company. And to top it all there is even 'The Homeland of Totoro', an area of the

Sayama hills preserved by the Totoro no Furusato Foundation – a charitable organisation dedicated to Japan's natural habitat. It secured its first land in 1991 (Totoro's Forest #1) and has expanded since, showing that Totoro's effect on a rapidly urbanising environment can make a difference. Miyazaki himself has supported the project.

The success of the film and the titular character emerged in the most unexpected but delightful and award-winning way in 2022. Featuring approved and adapted music from Joe Hisaishi (with Will Stuart) the musical stage adaptation of *My Neighbour Totoro* launched in 2022 in the UK. It was so successful that it broke the Barbican Theatre's opening box-office record and triumphed in, among others, the 2023 Laurence Olivier Awards where it received six awards and was nominated for three more. A delightful, magical and endearing family treat for the stage, it was reprised for the 2023/2024 season.

Kiki's Delivery Service (Majo no takkyūbin) (1989)

Written (screenplay) and directed by: Miyazaki Hayao

'I don't find flying that much fun, it's more of a job to me.'

Effervescent and eager witch-in-waiting Kiki follows the ancient traditions of her kind by leaving home at 13 to begin her transformation into fully fledged witch-hood. Aided and abetted by the faithful Jiji, a talkative and opinionated black cat, she sets out to find a suitable town where she can nurture her burgeoning talents. Money is tight, though, so it's especially convenient that she finds accommodation with the kindly, jovial baker Osono, who lets her stay in her flour-dusted attic room. Osono has a bun in the oven in the figurative as well as literal sense and welcomes the enthusiastic fledgling witch into her home. In order to make ends meet Kiki comes up with a business plan that will utilise her major talent – flying – and she starts up a service delivering parcels around town. The plan has teething troubles but soon Kiki and Jiji are welcomed into the community, and are especially popular with Tombo, a bespectacled boy whose greatest desire is to fly, and Ursula, an artist. However, Kiki faces her biggest challenge when her ability to fly seems to falter and a renegade dirigible threatens to plough into the very clock tower that drew her to the town in the first place, endangering the lives of those she has come to know.

Captivating and charming, *Kiki's Delivery Service* is a film that soars as high as its vibrant heroine and is as magical as her powers. Devoid of the gothic earnestness and big messages writ large of, say, the *Harry Potter* series, *Kiki's Delivery Service* explores a desire to be different through witchcraft in a way that is far more uplifting and ultimately human. This is, at heart, a children's film made for adults, one that appeals to the free spirit of childhood but which is so rich in themes and development that its apparent simplicity is deceptive. The essence of Miyazaki's films, as in *My Neighbour Totoro* and the altogether more nightmarish *Spirited Away*, is childlike but not childish. Based upon the children's book by Kadono Eiko, first published in 1985, *Kiki's Delivery Service* follows its heroine's first steps to witch-hood. Four further books about the plucky witch have been published since. Although the film generally follows events in the book there are substantial differences, particularly towards the film's set-piece finale. The literal title translates as 'The Witch's Express Home Delivery Company' – *Witch's Takkyūbin*. The *takuhaibin* service in Japan is an efficient and cheap form of door-to-door delivery, the most prominent of which is the *takkyūbin* service run by Yamato Transport. Their ubiquitous logo comprises a black mother cat carefully carrying her kitten in her mouth. The adoption of 'Takkyūbin' in the title caused no issues regarding trademark infringement.

The struggle between tradition and modernity, and between craft and technology, is a theme in many of Miyazaki's films, most notably *Princess Mononoke*, but never so eloquently argued as in *Kiki's Delivery Service*. The lament for the passing of the old together with an appreciation of the coming of the new provides the central theme of the film, both technologically and emotionally. Rather like Thomas Hardy viewing the decline of traditional agriculture in the wake of the rise of industrialism, Miyazaki views the new age as inevitable while acknowledging tradition. Kiki herself is not averse to modern living – she's perfectly happy listening to the radio while drifting in the night on her broomstick – but is sensitive to her heritage. She was brought up in a rural community, so while she observes the protocol that she must wear black, she does top her hair with a vivid crimson bow. When she helps an old lady bake a fish pie to take to her granddaughter's birthday party she does so by reigniting an old oven, the modern cooker having broken down – respect for aged machinery and people is seen as important. Kiki is always very polite and respectful, bowing and using honorific language to her elders, so it's galling when the recipient of the pie is dismissive and ungrateful. Comparisons between the old and new occur throughout the film and are most succinctly observed when Kiki is seen on her broomstick as a plane flies in the distance – tradition and modernity side by side. That Kiki's only genuine adversary is the strictly non-human dirigible creates further conflict between old and new. It is a dilemma that has also perplexed Studio Ghibli, which has, at times, struggled with the increasing ubiquity of CGI in contemporary animation. Studio Ghibli films are by their very nature handcrafted works of art; indeed, it is precisely this that makes them so rich and organic. Although some later Ghibli pictures have used CGI, indeed *Earwig and the Witch* was the studio's first full 3-D CGI production, their trust in traditional animation was what made their work so special.

Kiki's Delivery Service is also about emotional transition, the coming of puberty signalled by Kiki's departure from home to start life in the real world. In many ways it is about the loss of innocence at childhood's end, but the film also acknowledges adult life, and its responsibilities, as an inevitable outcome of the human condition. Kiki's first indication that adulthood is approaching comes when she has a fever and Jiji begins dating the fluffy white cat Lily, promptly losing the ability to speak. Jiji's feline sarcasm is a frequent delight throughout the film – 'The Ocean is huge!' squeals Kiki; 'Just a puddle to me,' responds Jiji drolly. His expressive eyes contribute to the film's most amusing sequences, such as when he is forced to act like a stuffed toy in a house with a large, slobbering dog called Jeff. When he becomes 'just' a cat, Kiki's despair is all too understandable; thereafter she fears that she is losing her powers and cannot fly. Her road to adulthood has begun. However, a number of female role models help her emerge as a woman and act as a replacement for her absent-but-caring mother. Osono is a good businesswoman. Ursula is independent and determined and acts as a mentor to the young witch, teaching her to be true to herself and to understand her limitations. Her admission that 'sometimes I can't paint a thing' helps Kiki realise that failings are inevitable, but that spirit and perseverance will triumph. Rather as William Morris suggests, the link between honest work and artistry is palpable and all to the social good. 'The spirit of witches. The spirit of artists. The spirit of bakers,' is perhaps the phrase that best sums up the blend of craftsmanship, artistry and magic that defines the films of Studio Ghibli. The visual metaphor can be seen in the sign for Kiki's Delivery Service itself, handcrafted by Osono's husband in salt dough.

Originally Miyazaki was only going to produce the film because of his heavy workload on *My Neighbour Totoro*, but eventually he decided to direct it as well because he couldn't find anyone else who was suitable for the project. It is difficult to see how anyone else could have realised the film. The animation is superb throughout – Kiki's flapping dress as she shoots through the sky, closely observed cows chewing straw, Tombo's attempts to fly using his modified bike and the droop-jawed lumbering of Jeff the dog. Equally impressive is the film's use of sound. Joe Hisaishi's varied and uplifting score underpins the film to perfection but it is in the climactic scenes that sound is used to best effect – by its absence. When Kiki faces her biggest challenge the sound just cuts dead as we wait, breathless, to see if she can succeed. It's a powerful moment that accentuates the tension of the scene.

Kiki's Delivery Service's combination of humour, adventure and self-discovery makes it close to being the perfect family film. Set in a European town of indeterminate location but resolutely Japanese in its execution, it is an uplifting film that revels in humanity and community spirit.

Only Yesterday (Omohide poro poro) (1991)

Written (screenplay) and directed by: Takahata Isao

Okajima Taeko, a hard-working Tōkyō office lady, has decided to take a break from the pressures of city life. Her aim is simple: to visit a rural haven that she can call home, if only for a week or so. As luck would have it, her sister's husband's family happens to own a farm in Yamagata so Taeko leaps at the opportunity of spending some time working in the fields. But somehow Taeko is constantly reminded of her life growing up as a girl in Tōkyō and begins to feel that her trip is awakening memories of a part of her life she cannot fully reconcile. Met at the station by Toshio, a relative of the person she was expecting to meet, she is driven to the little mountain farm, eager to get started. This turns out to be quite fortuitous for part of the farm's work is picking and processing safflower, a task suited to the early morning. The work is hard and relentless but its physicality, the natural open air and the unpretentious company of her co-workers make Taeko feel happy for the first time in many years. Observing this brief transformation is her early self, the young teenage girl whose life, loves and heartaches have created the woman she is today. But will the break lead to long-term contentment for Taeko, or will this be a fleeting glimpse of happiness preceding a return to the daily drudgery of office life? For, as an unmarried lady of 27, her chances of attaining some sort of domestic stability are slipping away.

In contrast to the more fantastical films of Studio Ghibli, *Only Yesterday* is a contemporary drama. On the surface this appears strange, as animation is a time-consuming and expensive way of realising a film that, for the most part, could have been shot with live actors. However, there are a number of reasons why *Only Yesterday* is more ideally suited to anime, not least of which is the total control that animation gives its creators. It is set in two time frames – the early 1980s as Japan was approaching the peak of its economic might, and 1966 when urbanisation was developing rapidly. Realising both these time periods would have been expensive in a live-action film and the way *Only Yesterday* merges the past and present could have caused logistical difficulties. For the most part it is stylised, a realistic sense of the film's 'now' contrasting with the less authentic 'realism' of 1966 without resorting to flashback clichés.

Takahata's script for *Only Yesterday* was derived from Okamoto Hotaru and Tone Yuko's nostalgic *josei manga* (comics designed for women), which feature vignettes from the life of an 11-year-old girl, Taeko, in the 1960s. The first volume was published in 1990 and is part of a long-running genre of 'little snippets of life' manga made famous by such Japanese institutions as *Sazae-san*. Rather like *My Neighbours the Yamadas*, Takahata's adaptation has to take short, episodic scenes and fashion them into an overarching narrative. With *Only Yesterday* Takahata links the nostalgic, innocent past to the present by having Taeko look back on her childhood, and in doing so adds an extra layer of poignancy to proceedings. In this respect, Takahata has departed from the source material but only in a way that makes it more coherent for a feature film. The manga's nostalgia for childhood and the trappings of the time – the music, the fashions – is given a wistful and melancholy air by demonstrating how not coming to terms with your past can affect the rest of your life. Takahata's take on the source material both comments on it and places it in the context of a wider whole. Crucially, though, when dealing with the vignettes of 1966 he remains faithful to the manga.

Although a poignant film filled with hope, *Only Yesterday* tempers its nostalgia with a sense of dreams unfulfilled and of a childhood that was marked by inaction. In many ways, Takahata's films are about imperfection and compromise; they affect their audience on an emotional level precisely because they mirror the truth. The artifice of animation takes on a wider universality because Takahata's characters are flawed but believable, the resolution of the film rarely resolving the story. As in *Pom Poko*, the conclusion of *Only Yesterday* is left open, perhaps looking to a better future, but maybe one with limitations. In this way Takahata seems to be saying that, yes, life is complicated, but we should be grateful for the little moments of happiness. In *Grave of the Fireflies* Seita refuses to act on the opportunities he is given, his inaction resulting in the death of his sister and ultimately himself. In *Only Yesterday* Taeko moves away from her job, if only briefly, to travel to the countryside. The film seems to indicate that her life between the 1960s and the 1980s has been wasted. Because of early family pressures and her own subsequent inactivity, she has remained bound to Japan's sprawling capital, and it is only when she actively makes a decision to escape her self-imposed concrete-and-neon prison that her early life can be free to express itself to her.

Although the 1966 childhood we are shown in *Only Yesterday* is tinged with nostalgia it nevertheless shows the deep frustrations that are part of growing up. In some sense Taeko's journey to Yamagata is the final stage of the process, and long overdue. She complains that in order to become a butterfly a caterpillar must first submit to the pupa state, a state that she has been in for over 15 years, her metamorphosis into full womanhood stagnated at adolescence. The key seems to be her constant wish to be free of the urban sprawl, something she glimpsed on a trip to an *onsen* (hot spring) resort. This is where the film speaks to people who grew up in the 1960s: the nostalgia boom in the Japanese entertainment industry, the rise in the 'Group Sounds' following the Beatles' first visit to Japan, Kenji 'Julie' Sawada and The Tigers, the hugely popular puppet show *Hyokkori Hyotanjima* and so on. Sprinkled throughout the film are songs from both the 1980s and the 1960s. And more than this, there is a universality about the way children cope with adolescence and learn how to deal with the opposite sex. *Only Yesterday* confronts adulthood frankly by addressing young Taeko's fears about approaching menstruation, a matter not made any easier by the boys' discovery of the girls' sex-education classes, which intensifies their natural curiosity. Taeko goes to great lengths to explain, when excused from PE because of a fever, that she is most definitely not having a period. But to no avail. The boys become obsessed with looking up the girls' skirts (a practice mirrored in Nagai Go's ground-breaking 1967 manga *Harenchi Gakuen*). When the fashion for mini-skirts arrives, young ladies are careful to cover their behinds with shopping bags when ascending escalators. It is this attention to detail that makes *Only Yesterday* such a rounded experience, combining the universal (growing up) with the specific (1966). 1966 saw Japan on the upturn and set the scene for its subsequent economic standing. This can be best illustrated in the scene where Taeko's father brings home a pineapple for the family to share – a hugely expensive item and a sign of the family's growing prosperity. However, as no one actually knows how to prepare the fruit, they have to wait to find out, watching in awe as Mother eventually slices and serves it with great ceremony. When the fruit is finally eaten, the family admit to disappointment at the end result. It is a disappointment that mirrors Taeko's life when her dreams of becoming an actress – and even, maybe, starring with her sister's favourite acting troupe, the Takarazuka – are coming to fruition, only to be shattered by her father's conservatism.

Only Yesterday takes pains to contrast the artificiality of the city with the honesty of the countryside, although Takahata, who refuses to make his films polemical, concedes that even a natural country lifestyle alters nature itself. The nostalgia in the film is really a lament for a dwindling agricultural sector, an attempt to reconcile Japan's desire for its countryside idyll with its desire for continued urban expansion. This is more than a modern struggle between the countryside and the city; it tries to get across the pain and resentment of the agricultural industry.

The film seeks to address the reasons why such bitterness exists through the character of Toshio. He explains the hardships faced by the country dwellers while driving his battered old car to the farm, placing the agricultural industry into a wider social context. Taeko may want to experience traditional farming but the young people who live in the countryside just want Puma trainers and an escape to the city. The job on the farm involves picking and processing safflower, a thistle-like plant used in the manufacture of rouge. Taeko wears gloves when picking the prickly flowers but briefly removes them to try and embrace the past – worker women of times gone by who picked the buds found their hands ripped to shreds. The red lips of the decadent ladies in Kyōto were literally stained with the blood of peasants.

Takahata seamlessly mixes the two pasts together, with Taeko occasionally even meeting her younger self. The two animation styles complement each other in a delicate but pronounced way and the temporal leaps are effortless. The 1980s are animated in a realistic style, etching out the lines on the faces of the characters or noting the perfect detail in a single head of safflower pollinated by a bee. The 1960s are shown in a more stylised manner with pastel, almost diffused edges to the frames, sketched out with items of memorabilia. For the most part *Only Yesterday* is so grounded in reality that, in the brief moments when it departs from realism, the effect is startling. When schoolgirl Taeko first experiences teenage romance she is so elated that she literally walks upwards into the clouds.

Only Yesterday was considered something of a gamble – devoid of any easy-to-market, advert-friendly fantasy presence it had to stand up on the basis of the quality of its writing. Ghibli would return to the drama format with *Ocean Waves*, *Whisper of the Heart* and *From Up on Poppy Hill*.

Porco Rosso (The Crimson Pig) (Kurenai no buta) (1992)

Written and directed by: Miyazaki Hayao

'Laws don't apply to pigs.'

Captain Marco Pagot – adventurer, pilot, free spirit, quick with his fists, quick to love. His name may well be Marco Pagot, but you can call him Porco Rosso, the Crimson Pig. Yes, for reasons that don't ever become crystal clear, the Captain is of a porcine nature, flying his bright-red plane from his island retreat to clear the air of pirates, even if this involves the danger of dodging the rat-a-tat of machine-gun fire. We first see our rugged hero saving a shipload of schoolgirls from being kidnapped by Mamma Aiuto's pirates, even negotiating with them to split the booty. But the threat of pirates becomes more pronounced when smarmy American rogue Curtis tries to broker an arrangement with the disparate group of scallywags at the flying club owned by Gina, an old friend of Marco's. Curtis wants to whisk Gina off to the US but she is holding out for the angst-ridden pig. Curtis challenges Marco, shooting him from the skies in a cowardly act and leaving him for dead. But it's not over for the pig-headed one. Aided and abetted by 17-year-old super-mechanic Fio Piccolo, who repairs his plane, he is ready to roam the air once more. Times, however, are changing. With the economy in depression there are dark tidings of a fascist uprising. Marco is forced to fight for those he loves against the man who hates him most.

The genesis of *Porco Rosso* is a strange and slightly unhinged one. Initially the film was financed by Japan Airlines as a flagship product for their in-flight entertainment; after all, what could be more prestigious than an exclusive film from such a revered animator? It's easy to see why the idea appealed to Miyazaki. It's a film about flying to be shown in planes – it seemed like perfect synergy (bar the fact, of course, that in-flight entertainment screens can hardly compete with their cinematic equivalents). Originally the film was going to be roughly 30-45 minutes long, presumably in order to be screened on domestic as well as international flights, but, as Miyazaki got into the project, the film became more expansive, took on more sponsors and became a feature-length production.

The creation of the central character was also unconventional. *Porco Rosso*'s actual name, Marco Pagot, is said to have come from an Italian animator who had worked with Miyazaki on *Sherlock Hound* some years before. For many years Miyazaki had been sporadically contributing to *Model Graphix* magazine, a specialist publication aimed at model enthusiasts, focusing on tanks, ships and aircraft but also mecha and other more fanciful items less grounded in the real world. Miyazaki's column generally consisted of deconstructing planes and tanks from the first half of the twentieth century (sometimes modified to reflect Miyazaki's own ideas about design) and short adventure strips featuring these vehicles. Many of the characters used in the column were anthropomorphised pigs but also included humans, some of whom look like the leader of Mamma Aiuto's pirates. The elements further gelled when he produced a three-part story, *Hikōtei Jidai* (*The Era of the Flying Boat*), in the early 1990s, which is, to all intents and purposes, a dry run of *Porco Rosso*, right down to the fisticuffs conclusion. Miyazaki's work for *Model Graphix* was later compiled into a lavish art book entitled *Hayao Miyazaki's Daydream Notes* and his later *The Wind Has Risen* manga for the magazine would become the basis for *The Wind Rises*. 'I have to admit that ever since I was a child, I, too, have been a fan of military planes, warships, and tanks,' Miyazaki said in his article for *Animation Monthly* in July 1980. The importance of planes in Studio Ghibli's work cannot be overemphasised. The company derived their name in part from an Italian aircraft that was used in World War Two and Marco himself flies a plane with a Ghibli engine.

In some respects, *Porco Rosso* is Miyazaki's most personal film. Undoubtedly *My Neighbour Totoro* contains elements that could be deemed autobiographical but *Porco Rosso* represents Miyazaki's obsessions and dreams. It unashamedly references animation's traditional and experimental past. Many Ghibli films have some elements of self-reflexivity in them (rather like the Pixar films, characters from other films sometimes crop up in the background), but *Porco Rosso* goes further by encompassing the works of pioneering animators, in a way that places the film very much in the first part of the twentieth century. This happens right from its opening, when the film is introduced in many different languages simultaneously, an almost identical technique to Norman McLaren's experimental animation *Hen Hop* (1942) – although McLaren didn't have his words revealed by marching *nandarou*, strange creatures that feature in Ghibli's celebratory TV spots for NHK. Later, Marco, being shadowed by a secret agent, enters a cinema. The film showing is clearly an homage to early Disney Mickey Mouse shorts as well as featuring Winsor McCay's charming *Gertie the Dinosaur* (1914), arguably the first hand-drawn, animated, anthropomorphised animal.

In common with many of Miyazaki's films, the female characters are notably capable and resourceful. Gina owns the club for pilots and yearns to be with loner Marco. She is prepared to wait for a romance that in all likelihood won't happen and tries to keep her business afloat in harsh economic times. Her own past, with three husbands dead through flying, has made her stronger, not a victim. This is the way that Miyazaki's women deal with any crisis – they buckle down and get on with life. Fio, likewise, is determined and resilient. She demands that Marco take her mechanical skills seriously when he is initially reluctant to take on a 17-year-old engineer. Naturally she proves an invaluable assistant, admonishing her boss for undisciplined bravura and running the risk of ending up like 'roast pork'. Rather like in *Princess Mononoke* the women prove to be more adept at collectively organised work and keeping their community together. Indeed, for a film so concerned with machismo and flying there are relatively few defined male characters, the men folk having been forced away from the town in order to seek employment at a time of depression. Miyazaki shows how harsh times can bring out the best in a community, and also the worst – his women club together for the greater good but, in the wider context of the film, there is the worrying emergence of nationalism. Although not explicitly stated in the film, events in *Porco Rosso* are loosely connected with real history and set in the late 1920s. The dilemma is one that faces most proponents of social-political ideology – when does good, productive, social, community-based work become reactionary, nationalistic and totalitarian?

Porco Rosso himself is one of Miyazaki's more enigmatic but charismatic creations. He is a complex loner who, perhaps because of the social-political dilemma facing Italy, has rejected the country, its laws and the human race as a whole. 'I'd rather be a pig than a fascist,' he declares. He is the epitome of the heroes of such aviation classics as *Wings* (1927) and particularly *Only Angels Have Wings* (1939), his dark romance with the deadly heavens alienating him from the people who love him. There's more than a touch of Ernest Hemingway about this character, particularly in the brutal fisticuffs with Curtis that sees the two fighters slugging it out in shallow water. But at heart Marco is a pilot, perhaps an alter ego for the aviation-obsessed Miyazaki, who is given ample opportunity to revel in scenes of flight and derring-do. And what scenes they are: acutely observed planes swooping around, unrestrained by gravity, cutting swathes through each other with deadly gunfire (although Marco, of course, doesn't stoop so low as to fire killing shots, even at his foes). Miyazaki clearly relishes these scenes although, technically, they are fiendishly difficult to animate as they occur in a 3-D space whereas the bulk of cel animation traditionally restricts itself to planar 2-D spaces. When realising these sorts of scenes – be it the car chase of *The Castle of Cagliostro* or the flying scenes of *Laputa: Castle in the Sky* – Miyazaki often uses a forced, curved, perspective when emphasising 3-D movement to get a sense of urgency and acceleration. With the open skies and blue seas of *Porco Rosso*, however, he can engage in far more free-form flight with dramatic results. His creativity at animating flight would find its zenith in *The Wind Rises*.

Porco Rosso is a dynamic action adventure in the mould of classic Hollywood films by the likes of Howard Hawks and John Huston, with a darker subtext than most of Miyazaki's output. It is one of his few films for Ghibli that doesn't contain a notable environmental message. It became the number one box-office hit of its year.

Ocean Waves (Umi ga kikoeru) (1993)

Directed by: Mochizuki Tomomi

Yutaka and Taku become friends when they turn out to be the only two students willing to sustain a protest about the cancellation of a school trip. Taku has a lot on his plate, trying to maintain university entrance grades, but he also works as a dishwasher for an ex-*yakuza* chef so that he can afford to go on a later school trip to Hawaii. Although they never share the same class, Yutaka and Taku form a bond, especially when Yutaka develops a crush on Rikako, a mid-term transfer from Tōkyō. Rikako seems to have it all – exceptional grades, great sports skills and stunning good looks, her city sophistication exotic to the teenagers in Kōchi, a coastal city on the island of Shikoku. But snooty Rikako finds it hard to adapt and wants to return to Tōkyō to live with her estranged father. On the Hawaii trip she claims to have lost her money and coerces a blushing Taku to lend her a sizeable amount. It later transpires that she is trying to get enough money to return to Tōkyō, which she does, with Taku as an escort, but only because Rikako's only friend Yumi pulls out of the trip at the last minute. News of their journey together spreads around the school and before long friendships become strained to breaking point.

A further example of Ghibli's determination not to be shoehorned into specific genres, *Ocean Waves* is a bitter-sweet, coming-of-age romantic drama that explores the emotional tensions within a group of youngsters on the threshold of adulthood. It marked something of a departure for the studio in that neither Miyazaki nor Takahata directed, although Takahata oversaw the production as producer. In order to prepare the company for the future, Ghibli used the project as a way of encouraging and empowering their younger animators. They brought in director Mochizuki Tomomi, maker of popular telekinetic high-school romance series *Kimagure Orange Road*, among others. *Ocean Waves* (the Japanese title literally translates as *I Can Hear the Sea*) also marked Ghibli's first foray into television programming. However, the film's eventual cost, above the projected modest budget, meant that they would later rethink this strategy. They would not produce another TV programme for seven years and that was to be the 12-minute *Ghiblies*, not a feature-length film. Based on the book by Himuro

Saeko that was illustrated by Kondō Katsuya (one of Ghibli's key animators who also worked on the film version), *Ocean Waves* is a slight but sweet tale of romance and friendship.

The high-school romance is a popular part of Japanese literature and manga, especially in *shōjo*, comics aimed at girls. *Ocean Waves* is unusual in that the romance is seen through the eyes of Taku, but doesn't feature the overt comedy often associated with versions of the genre marketed for boys. While it doesn't lack humour or scenes of lechery (the boys go goggle-eyed at the girls playing tennis), the dramatic tension and need to come to terms with the emotional rites of passage make it more melodramatic and thoughtful. The film succeeds at portraying this drama as a nostalgia piece, and it is mainly constructed as a series of flashbacks as Taku recalls his past on a flight to Tōkyō. Unlike *Only Yesterday*, which uses a similar structure, *Ocean Waves*' events are separated by no more than a couple of years rather than decades. The characters have grown up so much in a short space of time that even the recent past seems a distant memory

The catalyst for the story is Rikako. She is doubly mysterious to Taku – firstly, she's a girl and, secondly, an outsider. Her mid-term arrival is something of a rarity for the school; she has been forced to move because of a messy divorce between her parents, something for which she blames her mother. Having left Tōkyō, the sprawling metropolis of nearly 13 million people, she finds herself in Kōchi, a small city about the size of Coventry, on the island of Shikoku, far from mainland Honshu. Her otherness is marked out in many ways – she is stylishly dressed, worldly and, above all, her accent is distinctly different. Part of her early inability to communicate is that she finds it hard to understand what people are saying to her; 'Kōchi-ben reminds me of samurai films, I thought dialects were lost,' she notes, her Tōkyō-based life and exposure to NHK (standard) Japanese having left her at a disadvantage in this new environment. It doesn't help when Taku points out to her that Tōkyō-ben is 'harsh', one of many interactions highlighting the painful misunderstandings between the two. Taku is justifiably annoyed when he learns that Rikako has lied in order to get him to lend her money, but he still accompanies her to Tōkyō in order to save Yumi from being admonished by her mother. Rikako's lies reflect the cynicism of the 'sophisticated' city and contrast with the relative innocence of Kōchi. Her selfishness comes back to haunt her when she finds out that her father has taken a mistress, changed her old bedroom and that her boyfriend Okada has dumped her.

For a TV animation, *Ocean Waves* is beautifully produced, with strong attention to detail and striking use of perspective. It has an unusual flashback motif where photo frames from the past influence the present. Although not in the same league as its big-screen cousins, *Ocean Waves* is still an enjoyable drama.

Pom Poko (Heisei tanuki gassen pompoko) (1994)

Written and directed by: Takahata Isao
Concept by: Miyazaki Hayao

> *'Tanuki tanuki will you come out and play?*
> *I can't, I'm eating now.*
> *What are you eating?*
> *Pickled plums and radish.'*

The Tama New Town Project, started in 1966, is a wonderful urban development that reflects Japan's growing prosperity. Years later, the economic boom of the 1980s identifies a need to further develop Tōkyō's suburbs for the next generation. A flourishing time for all? Perhaps not. The Tama New Town

In hot pursuit – car capers in *The Castle of Cagliostro*

Gōshu's cello practice is disturbed by an inquisitive cat in *Gōshu the Cellist*

Nausicaä seeks answers in *Nausicaä of the Valley of the Wind*

Pazu and Sheeta meet a Laputan robot in *Laputa: Castle in the Sky*

Siblings Seita and Setsuko share a fleeting moment of happiness in *Grave of the Fireflies*

Surveying the countryside in *My Neighbour Totoro*

A pandemonium of parakeets are positively petrifying in *The Boy and the Heron*

Kiki and Jiji wait for customers in *Kiki's Delivery Service*

Rural idyll in *Only Yesterday*

Captain Marco Pagot. Ace pilot. All pig. *Porco Rosso*

Tanuki courtship in *Pom Poko*

An impromptu rendition of *Country Roads* in *Whisper of the Heart*

Ready for battle. *Princess Mononoke*

My Neighbours the Yamadas

The strange and terrifying world of *Spirited Away*

Itadakimasu! Sōsuke and Ponyo are ready for ramen in *Ponyo on the Cliff by the Sea*

Shun gives Umi a ride to the shops and buys her a snack in *From Up on Poppy Hill*

Princess Kaguya is delighted by the beautiful blossoms

Project has been a cause of concern for the local *tanuki* as their forest lands diminish and the once harmonious coexistence they have enjoyed with humans starts disappearing in a waft of consumerism and urban sprawl. This causes tension between the *tanuki* of Suzuka and Takaga forests who battle fiercely for what little territory remains. Grandma Oroku knows best, though, and wisely advises them to bury their differences to concentrate on the greater problem – the humans.

The fun-loving *tanuki* agree, somewhat begrudgingly, to a five-year plan whereby they will work at reawakening their long-dormant transformation skills in order to defeat the humans. Training commences but soon the group realise that old differences are more than territorial; they are ideological. Gonta wants to lead a revolt to attack the humans while Shōkichi's group are more in favour of a compromise where humans and *tanuki* live together, as they did in the days before the bulldozers arrived. After all, the humans do have delicious food. However, it soon becomes apparent that more drastic action needs to be taken – Oroku has demanded a strict chastity policy to prevent population growth while two top *tanuki*, Tamasaburo and Bunta, are sent out to Shikoku and Sado to seek the masters of transformation who can hopefully save the forests. Despite some high-profile media reports of *tanuki* sabotage, the development is carrying on regardless and time is running out.

Tanuki have long held a strong place in the folklore of Japan. Mischievous, fun-loving, amoral characters, they are wish fulfilment on four legs – always partying and having a good time like a salaryman out on the town following a particularly successful deal. As *Pom Poko* explains, though, their key skill lies in the ability to transform into whatever they wish, should they be gifted enough. Chameleons, we are told, are at the rudimentary end of the scale, rank amateurs at best, while the true masters of the form are foxes and *tanuki*. Oh, and some cats, as we shall later see in *The Cat Returns*. The difference with *tanuki* is that they are so hell bent on a life of ease and hedonism that they are prone to laziness and their habitat dwindles away because of the march of human industrialism. In most Ghibli films there is a debate about the attitudes of the past and those of the present, and an examination of the ways in which the environment has been squandered. *Pom Poko* is no exception, looking back to a time when humans and *tanuki* lived in harmony, decrying the current generation for their consumerism and looking for grains of hope in the future.

The *tanuki* are swift to revel in any victory, however minor, using their robust bellies as drums to beat out dance music. But there is a sense that they are fiddling while Rome burns, denying the evidence before their eyes. They know that they must obey Grandma Oroku when she tells them to abstain from breeding, but once spring is in the air they just can't help it. Even the morally upright Shōkichi and Okiyo become passionate mates – after a sweet courtship, of course. Passion is natural and the *tanuki* show that their natural instincts can only be put on hold for so long. Part of this is manifested in the male *tanuki*'s most prominent assets – his testicles. Testicles play an important role in *tanuki* mythology but they are more than just a fertility symbol. They feature in a number of traditional rhymes, one of the most popular of which roughly translates as '*Tanuki* balls still swing even when there's no wind'. Indeed, the *kanji* characters for testicles are gold and ball(s) in vernacular Japanese, pointing to the animal as lucky or prosperous. In *Pom Poko*, the *tanuki*'s testicles are put to a variety of uses – disguises, makeshift parachutes, and they are even blown up to an unfeasible size to make a space-hopper-style bouncing weapon that emits a bagpipe-like drone.

For a non-Japanese audience *Pom Poko* can seem overwhelming in its cultural references, including both Shintō and Buddhist imagery, the latter depicted particularly in the *tanuki* ship to the afterlife. Cultural and mythological lore is brought to the fore when the *tanuki* launch their assault on the humans – 'The Spooking War' – in which they attempt to get rid of people by transforming themselves into ghost figures and scaring them. During the marching parade, overseen by huge spectral shadows cast on the sides of tower blocks, the *tanuki* transform into a variety of mischievous spirits, or *yōkai*. In the great parade a whole pantheon of creatures is unleashed: giant carps and dragons, *karakasa* and *rokurokubi* (humans with long, snake-like necks) among many others. A number of these are seen in an extended long shot where two drunken men at a food stall discuss the possibility of the existence of supernatural beings, patently ignoring the mayhem around them. If you're really observant, you'll spot a bunch of other Ghibli characters, including Totoro on his spinning top, Kiki on her broom and Porco Rosso, as the transformed *tanuki* fly through the air towards the parade.

As humans reject their natural environment, nature's choices are shown to be either rebellion or acquiescence. In the case of the more devious *kitsune*, or foxes, the similarities to humankind are all too apparent – they have become virtually human, revelling in a society that offers them untold consumerist riches. Kitsune Ryutaro tries to broker a deal between the *tanuki* and the owner of the Wonderland theme park at his hostess club in trendy Ginza. His argument is simple – if you can't beat 'em, join 'em: transform into human shape and bring home the paycheque. But not all *tanuki* can transform and therein lies the dilemma – succumb to the inevitable while realising that this means the weaker will die along with their habitat.

The film uses the animation process to portray the complex way in which the *tanuki* exist through metamorphosis. We are told early on that *tanuki* are naturally bipedal, only reverting to quadruped form when humans are present. In the quadruped state the *tanuki* are animated to match their familiar, real-life appearance. Once bipedal, they are portrayed in a number of distinct styles, from stylised, obviously anime characters, to traditional woodblock representations, to full-blown human form. Clothes come and go depending on the circumstances and situation, often changing in the blink of an eye. The tired or scared *tanuki* reverts to his non-human look very quickly, so it is imperative to be vigilant at all times. What marks the animation in *Pom Poko* is the way that the film so effortlessly segues between these states, from naturalistic to stylised anthropomorphism, one step further on from the creatures of *Gōshu the Cellist*. This fluidity of style would reach its zenith in *The Tale of Princess Kaguya*. As with *Gōshu*, though, there is a clear indication as to where the anthropomorphism stops and the animal characteristics come back. There is a link between mammals but a clear delineation between the species – Ryutaro may look human but he's still a wily fox; Shōkichi may become a salaryman but he still throws off his outer look to return to the hedonistic embrace of his natural *tanuki* community.

The film's conclusion offers bitter compromise – not the annihilation of the whole environment and the decimation of the species but a subjugation that involves rustling around waste bins and trying to avoid the deadly traffic. Only little havens of green land remain to remind the urbanites that there was once something other than concrete and glass. The *tanuki*'s bloody last stance, with its piles of corpses, sees those defeated take a treasure boat to the other world, singing and partying all the way. Those remaining use their abilities to transform the Tama

New Town Project into a lush green landscape, if only for a few beautiful moments.

Pom Poko is a glorious film full of *joie de vivre* and humour but it also mourns a past that cannot be reclaimed. The mixture of folk songs, rhymes and mythology makes for an exuberant film that offers just a glimmer of hope in that young children, rebelling against their parents' greed and myopia, may once more see a better world. The humanity in Takahata's films is perhaps most apparent when his protagonists are not human and *Pom Poko* is a perfect illustration of what animation can achieve and live action can only aspire to.

Whisper of the Heart (Mimi wo sumaseba) (1995)

Directed by: Kondō Yoshifumi
Written by: Miyazaki Hayao

Avid reader and burgeoning writer Tsukishima Shizuku is having a tough time balancing her life; with her father working at the library and her mother trying to finish her thesis, Shizuku and her sister have to deal with the household chores. The end-of-year exams are approaching and she desperately needs good grades in order to attend a decent high school. And then, of course, there are boys – desirable, stupid, talented and infuriating, often at the same time. Shizuku has a mystery to solve too. Every time she takes a book out of the library she notices that the name Amasawa Seiji appears on the lending card. Who can he be?

En route to deliver her father's lunchtime bento box she is accompanied on the train by a rather rotund cat, mostly creamy-grey coloured, but with a distinguishing brown left ear. Intrigued by the commuting kitty she follows it and chances upon an enticing antiques shop that sits incongruously among the suburban quiet of the town. The owner is Nishi Shirō, a kindly old man with an impish twinkle in his eye, who introduces her to the wonders of his shop, including the recently restored statuette of the Baron, a noble, aristocratic, bipedal cat with top-hat, tails and a cane. However, her astonishment is stretched to incredulity when she discovers that the most infuriating boy at her school is Nishi's grandson, a burgeoning violinmaker and frequenter of her beloved library.

Rather like *Only Yesterday*, *Whisper of the Heart* has the feel of a drama that, barring a few short sequences, could just as easily be served up as a live-action film. Anime embraces a far wider spectrum of genres than the more narrowly focused Western cartoon model, and *Whisper of the Heart*'s dense, rich plotting and characterisation would be difficult to realise so succinctly were the film not animated. It's a challenging blend, the apparently laid-back pacing a complete contrast to the runaway train of Shizuku's emotions. Key to gluing these elements together is perhaps the most unlikely of adhesives – the John Denver song 'Take Me Home, Country Roads' (written by John Denver, Bill Danoff and Taffy Nivert). The song is reprised, revised and alluded to throughout the film and marks Shizuku's growing confidence as a writer. Shizuku has been adapting the song for her school's choral society, revising it at each turn until she is satisfied with the results. Her confidence is dashed when Seiji gently mocks her first draft, 'Concrete Road', which alludes to the urbanisation of her surroundings, but this ultimately provides the basis for their initially exasperating relationship. Later the pair are joined by Nishi-san and his elderly friends in a delightful impromptu rendition of the track in the workshop basement of Nishi's shop. The evolution of 'Take Me Home, Country Roads' in *Whisper of the Heart* also reinforces Nishi's explanation of the process of artistry, of first having the germ of an idea – like a beryl buried in mica slate – but needing to expose and work with it to realise its true beauty. 'You and

Seiji,' he notes, 'are like this stone, rough and unpolished, still natural' to which Shizuku anxiously responds, 'What if there isn't a beautiful crystal inside me?'

In many ways, *Whisper of the Heart* is the most introspective of Ghibli's films in that it looks at the process of creativity and artistry, rather than concentrating on the results of those endeavours. The film returns to a key image, a woodcut illustration of a violinmaker locked in a prison cell practising his trade, showing the pull between the need to create and the self-imposed prison that this creativity demands. Art reflects life but also embellishes it. Shizuku fashions her novel from the story of the Baron and his painful separation from companion statue Luisa – their love a tragedy of loss. She has no way of knowing that Nishi's life mirrors that of the Baron in more ways than one, but empathises with the notion that the Baron lived in a fantastical land where 'in the veins of its artisans flowed the blood of sorcerers' – a joyous perception. Again, craft and art are seen as equally noble professions, the skills of a novelist or lyricist to be admired as much as those of a violinmaker or a violinist. Creativity is to be celebrated in all its forms. A further nod to the way in which this is a film about the creative process lies with the numerous Ghibli references that are peppered throughout the film – a Kiki-like witch doll, a *Porco Rosso* clock, a Totoro doll.

Cats play a vital role in shaping the world of *Whisper of the Heart*, although they would become even more central in the later related film *The Cat Returns*. Shizuku ultimately begins her journey as a writer because of the free-spirited cat she follows. She finds out that the cat has many names depending on which part of town he travels through. But to her he is known as 'Moon'. The observant but mute Moon is seen overlooking the city at the opening of the film. Also looking outward, immobile inside the antique shop, is another cat, Baron Humbert von Jikkingen. Although he plays a minor role, and could even be described as a MacGuffin, the character of the Baron holds the emotional key to the film's core, despite the fact that he is a small, inanimate statue. His presence provides the inspiration for Shizuku's novel. He becomes a charitable guide when the film briefly enters the realms of the fantastic – Shizuku's daydreams blended into the words of her story. These scenes are stylistically removed from the elegantly observed and detailed real world that forms the bulk of the main film. The fantasy sequence comprises colourful, acrylic, almost pointillist, landscapes of the surreal. The backdrops were created by Ōsakan painter Inoue Naohisa, whose works are often set in a utopian fantasy world he created called 'Iblard'. Indeed, they also formed the basis of the experimental Ghibli film of the same name. The Ghibli Museum short film *The Day I Harvested a Star* is also based upon his work.

Whisper of the Heart further examines Ghibli's recurring theme of struggle between the love of the traditional and the acceptance of modernity. At the centre of the film is the love of books, of writing and reading. This is relevant to Shizuku's family; her mother is finishing her thesis, her father works in the library and their small family home is crammed with piles of tomes. They are not averse to technology but are aware of the way progress can drain the soul from the things they hold dear. For Shizuku, this is encapsulated in a small but relevant change – the library is moving to a computerised system of registering and cataloguing their books which means that the stamped cards on the books' inside covers – with their history of former readers – will be replaced by a barcode. Shizuku and her compatriots are looking to the future but a healthy respect for Nishi's generation means that tradition will be maintained, if slightly changed. Nishi's generation represents hands-on craftsmanship – the beauty of his mechanical grandfather clock with its intricate model miners – over the mass production of the modern age.

Whisper of the Heart is the only feature film directed by Kondō Yoshifumi, a talented animation director, designer and artist who had worked on *Lupin III*, *Conan, the Boy in Future* and *Anne of Green Gables* as well as producing character designs for *Sherlock Hound*. He joined Ghibli in 1987 and worked on almost all their productions from *Grave of the Fireflies* to *Princess Mononoke* before sadly dying of an aneurysm in 1998, aged just 47. His importance to Ghibli was considerable. Although many commentators naturally focus on Miyazaki and Takahata, all the Studio Ghibli films are collaborative efforts – albeit with an unusually small team of workers for such high-quality films.

Although directed by Kondō, the collaboration with Miyazaki is also clear; indeed Miyazaki was closely involved with the brief but sublime fantasy sequences featuring the Baron, smoothing the contrast between these flights of fancy and the down-to-earth realism of Kondō's more restrained style. Miyazaki also provided the film's script and storyboards, adapted from the 1989 manga by Hiiragi Aoi, most famous for her *Hoshi no Hitomi no Silhouette* stories. Hiiragi would return to her Baron character in *Baron, Neko no Danshaku* (2002), a semi-sequel that was made into a film by Ghibli – *The Cat Returns*.

Princess Mononoke (Mononoke-hime) (1997)

Directed by: Miyazaki Hayao

'Can't humans and the forest live together in peace?'

Ashitaka may well be a hero, saving his village from the monstrous ravaging of an incensed, insane, poisonous boar-god, but his victory comes at a terrible price. With his arm infected by the beast, Ashitaka faces a death sentence, for the poison will seep into his bones and eventually he will die. The only solution for him, and ultimately his fellow villagers, the Emishi, is to travel west to discover what turned the boar-god into such a ferocious monster. The Emishi worry that their lives are under threat from the increasing unrest and violence emanating from the west. Ashitaka's journey bears witness to this, with hordes of samurai invading neighbouring villages. His attempts at intervention increase the power of the poison running through his veins but also provide him with immense physical strength. The outcome of the skirmishes is chaos; he sees a group of wolves, one with a girl riding on its back, being shot at by armed men led by an imposing woman in a red hat. Later he comes across wounded men on the outskirts of Deer Forest and, led by helpful, clicking *kodama* spirits, traverses the land 'where no man treads', sighting Shishigami (the Deer God/Forest Spirit). He returns the men, who are ox-drivers, to their home, a huge iron foundry fortress ruled by Lady Eboshi, the woman he has seen firing at the wolves earlier. Eboshi is at war with the land in order to manufacture weapons using its iron. She also faces a war with samurai keen to seize their assets, as well as the small but deadly entourage of terrorists led by Moro the wolf-god and Moro's adopted daughter San. Ashitaka is fascinated by San but also feels an affinity with the people of Eboshi. He faces the difficult task of trying to prevent as much bloodshed as possible while uncovering the cause of the sickness that is threatening the land.

Princess Mononoke became the most successful film released in Japan up until that time (it was beaten at the box office by James Cameron's all-conquering *Titanic* a few months later) and launched Ghibli on to the worldwide stage, introducing it to a more mainstream audience that stretched beyond the already enthusiastic world fan-base. Its success outside Japan was partly due to a deal with Disney that saw the film widely distributed on video, and, briefly, in cinemas, albeit dubbed. The film was distributed under their Miramax label – a film as violent as *Princess Mononoke* would not be released as a Disney film until *Pirates of the Caribbean* (2003). Miramax had originally wanted cuts to avoid a PG-13 rating but Miyazaki's staunch 'no cuts' policy forced them to capitulate. In many ways the film was a baptism of fire for Western viewers unfamiliar with anime, for *Princess Mononoke* is a rich and complex fantasy that offers no simple solutions and characters that are not wholly good or evil.

At heart, *Princess Mononoke* is a film about environmentalism and spirituality. Although concerned with humankind's rape of the countryside it nevertheless grudgingly admits that there are inevitably going to be conflicts between technological advancement and life in the wild. Indeed, you can almost feel the dilemma within the film itself because *Princess Mononoke* used computer technology to speed up production when the exorbitant number of cels needed to perfect Miyazaki's exacting vision required colouring – thus questioning the balance between craft and industrialisation. For both the physical film and its story, the battle resolved itself in the same way – traditional is best but progress is inevitable. At the centre of this battle is Eboshi's iron manufacturing town, its smoke-billowing smelting factories polluting the air, its deforestation programme leaving the countryside barren. The quest for iron, radically altered from its original form to create weapons, scars the land. The advantage offered by these weapons is clear: an untrained hand can become as deadly as that of a skilled warrior. Ashitaka's skilful way with a bow and arrow becomes increasingly obsolete in the shadow of progress. Indeed it is a bullet from one of Lady

Eboshi's own guns that has caused the rancour to spread in the boar-god, ultimately leading to Ashitaka's quest.

Less ambiguous is the film's relationship with spirituality, for it is through respect for the spirit world that true humanity is gained. This is shown early in the film when Ashitaka defeats the boar-god. Despite the fact that the beast brought pestilence and threatened to destroy their homes, the village Oracle still bows respectfully to the dying monster and apologises profusely. In contrast, Eboshi is seen as almost disdainful of the spirit world, viewing it as a hindrance to her goals; rather than mourn the death of a god, she actively seeks to destroy Moro and boar god Nago. Even more extreme is the attitude of the (unseen) Mikado, whose spies infiltrate Lady Eboshi's stronghold in order to decapitate Shishigami, whose head, the emperor believes, will grant him immortality. Interestingly, all the parties fervently believe in the spirit world – it is visible all around them; it is their attitudes that separate them – revering it, hating it, or viewing it as a commodity. If *My Neighbour Totoro* shows how deference to spirits can lead to a harmonious coexistence between worlds then *Princess Mononoke* shows what happens when they come into conflict, with results that are not pretty. Not that the *kami* are without internal conflict themselves – the red-eyed apes, in particular, offer a different kind of defiance against the humans, disagreeing with Moro and attempting to reverse the situation by planting trees where Lady Eboshi's men have felled them.

What is so striking about *Princess Mononoke* is the way that its characters, particularly its female characters, are such rounded and complex figures. Lady Eboshi, on the surface, would appear to be the villain of the story – after all, she is destroying the forest and is actively aggressive. But she also uses her position to help find employment for lepers, a maligned part of society, and also prostitutes whom she has saved from the brothels. These women provide further examples of earthy, working-class women in Miyazaki's films – spirited, capable individuals full of ribaldry and spunk. And then there's San, Princess Mononoke herself (a *mononoke* is the spirit of a thing – it can be responsible for all sorts of surprising, unexplained events which can be trivial or major). She's a wild free spirit, a cross between Kipling's Mowgli and Boudica. Her hatred of all humankind, which she sees as destructive of the forest and the natural order of things, has seen her reject any notion that she is human at all. She is the 'daughter' of Moro and has nothing but contempt for her own race. When we, and Ashitaka, first see her close up, she is sucking infected blood from Moro's side – he has been shot by one of Lady Eboshi's guns – her gore-streaked face showing nothing but confidence and hatred. Ashitaka is smitten, but getting through to this almost feral girl proves no easy matter. She finally accepts him on account of his worthiness, and that of his people, relayed to her by Ashitaka's faithful steed Yakul.

In terms of stretching the art of animation, *Princess Mononoke* is an astonishing achievement, especially given the sheer scale of the project and Miyazaki's hands-on approach to his films – personally reviewing, adjusting or creating nearly 80,000 of the film's 144,000 cels during the three years it took to make. Ghibli had a lot riding on *Princess Mononoke*, especially given the high cost of production. The results of this labour are present in every frame, from the stunning opening, where Ashitaka fights the boar-god, a tangle of diseased, morphing flowers of rancid flesh that undulate and attack with precision, to the wrath of the decapitated Shishigami that threatens to engulf the land. These scenes of high intensity, the skirmishes between factions, the hunting of the wolves, are countered by closely observed detail: the Hokusai-like day-to-day workings of Eboshi's people or the rustling of the wind through the grassy plains. The film's most haunting moments occur in the forest as beams of light prick through the hazy air and the soulful *kodama* click their heads, the majestic Shishigami silhouetted in the distance. The woodland setting for the film was inspired by the primeval forests of Yakushima, one of the Ōsumi Islands, located south of the island of Kyūshū. The sheer intensity of the workload on *Princess Mononoke* took its toll on Miyazaki. Exhausted, he announced that the film was to be his last as director. But he would return with *Spirited Away*.

Princess Mononoke is proof that animation can be as sophisticated and complex as any live-action piece, a truly adult film tackling relevant social issues while delivering an exciting story. Its box-office success was proof that treating your audience as mature viewers can reap rewards. It subsequently went on to win Best Film at the Japanese Academy Awards, the first time an animated feature was even nominated for the award.

My Neighbours the Yamadas
(Hōhokekyo tonari no Yamada-kun) (1999)

Written (screenplay) and directed by: Takahata Isao

Introducing my neighbours – the Yamada family. There's grandmother Shige and her occasionally work-shy housewife-daughter Matsuko. Matsuko and her salaryman husband Takashi have a son called Noboru and a daughter, Nonoko. And then there's Pochi the dog, usually found slouching in his kennel with an air of bemusement about him. All in all a pretty normal family. Well, sort of. The Yamadas, you see, have a problem in that everyday incidents can turn into seemingly insurmountable crises, normally as a result of an absentmindedness that either runs in the family or has something to do with the ginger they grow. Leaving Nonoko in the department store becomes a major kidnapping crisis, while the thought of separating out the weekly rubbish turns into a clandestine mission to fly-tip in public waste bins under the cloak of darkness. Takashi has all the salaryman problems but little of the salaryman income, finding life difficult whether it's bonding with his son or trying to negotiate for an umbrella in the midst of a torrential downpour. Matsuko, meanwhile, has to find increasingly devious ways of minimising the time spent in front of the stove. And then there are problems with the local *bōsōzoku* (biker gang) who will insist on revving their engines in the middle of the night. But can the Yamada family pluck up the courage to face them head on?

In tackling *My Neighbours the Yamadas* Takahata set himself the seemingly impossible task of producing a screenplay from a difficult source. *My Neighbours the Yamadas* is Ishii Hisaichi's hugely popular *yonkoma* manga (a four-cell comic strip) – the Western equivalent would be something like *Peanuts* or *Dilbert* – a quick-fire format that is difficult to translate into a feature-length film due to its episodic nature. The series began in 1991 in the newspaper *Asahi Shimbun*, Japan's second-largest circulation daily, as *My Neighbours the Yamadas*. The strip eventually began to focus on the daughter Nonoko and the title was changed to *Nono-chan* (*chan* being a term of endearment often suffixed to a child's name). The strip continues to be published to this day and even resulted in an anime TV series that ran for over 60 episodes on TV Asahi. Takahata's film wisely concentrates on all the family, allowing the format to develop in scope. This was a huge undertaking in terms of the way the film was structured – keeping audience interest in a series of what are basically vignettes, with little overriding narrative arc, while maintaining the look and feel of the original comic strips. Aesthetically, *My Neighbours the Yamadas* is quite unlike any other large studio animation. Takahata insisted that the film be true to the manga visually as well as in tone, not an easy task given that the original strip is highly stylised and sketchy. A similar dilemma on *Downtown Story* resulted in a simplification of the original manga designs due to time and budget limitations. Maintaining the style was difficult to realise using traditional cel animation, so the team looked at creating *My Neighbours the Yamadas* using digital painting techniques, allowing for pastel-shaded colours and watercolour backgrounds. It is hugely ironic that computer technology was required to imitate the simplicity of the original source material. Both Takahata and Miyazaki were deeply impressed by Frédéric Back's Oscar-winning short animation *Crac* (1980), a story that follows the history of a community through the perspective of a rocking chair that was carved from a tree. The distinctively drawn style and perspective of the animation finding its form and movement had a profound influence on the Yamadas, from the exhilaration of the dance sequences to the integration of distinct crowds of people around the central protagonist(s), as well as a story that commented on the impact of technology and time on its setting.

Rather like *Pom Poko*, *My Neighbours the Yamadas* is a film that balances its comic moments with ones of the utmost seriousness. Like *The Simpsons* it is essentially a comedy about an outwardly dysfunctional family but one that ultimately sticks together against the odds. Where it differs from its US counterpart, however, is the way in which cultural aspects are foregrounded to a much greater degree. The Yamadas have centuries of Japanese tradition behind them and this, whatever their individual foibles, affects every aspect of their lives. While *The Simpsons* makes passing reference to popular culture and occasionally US history, the Yamadas don't just comment on their past and surroundings, they embody them. Occasionally this can feel a little jarring in that Takahata will cut from a moment of comedy and segue into the next vignette by way of an illuminated *haiku* from poets such as Buson or Bashō. But this is deliberate, linking the modern-day Yamadas, with their video games and convenience food, to a rich tradition in art and culture. Nowhere is this link more apparent than in the rollercoaster flashback as to how the family came to be – a madcap wedding on a bobsleigh which transforms into a ship that is dwarfed by a huge wave reminiscent of *The Great Wave off Kanagawa*, the most internationally famous of Hokusai's *Thirty-six Views of Mount Fuji* series of prints. The couple 'conceive' their children by finding Noboru inside a peach and Nonoko in a bamboo shoot – both variations of popular folk tales, Noboru's 'birth' being based on *Momotarō*, the peach boy who grows up to fight demons, and Nonoko's on the *The Tale of the Bamboo Cutter* (*Taketori Monogatari*), which was, of course, the story that Takahata's next film, *The Tale of the Princess Kaguya*, was based upon. The film is sprinkled with allusions to Japanese paintings, folklore and writing as well as popular culture. When Takashi (finally and reluctantly) confronts the biker gang that have been raucous and noisy he gains strength from imagining himself as Gekko Kamen (Moonlight Mask), one of Japan's first TV superheroes. In many ways, this makes *My Neighbours the Yamadas* one of Ghibli's most difficult films to watch outside Japan, as every scene relies on cultural knowledge to fully engage with it. A chief source of amusement is the way that Matsuko occasionally flaunts etiquette and realises her errors but shrugs her shoulders anyway because, frankly, she's saved herself some effort. These moments range from the accidental (worried that she's left the kettle on or running through her house in her shoes, leaving a trail of muddy footprints) to the devious (contriving a situation where her son will inadvertently cook *ramen* [noodles] for her) as she aims to do as little as possible while staying within the remit of her role as housewife. She even gets the family around the table to enjoy *nabe* (a meal cooked at the table by the participants) and serves up a traditional Japanese breakfast to her grateful husband... until he realises it consists entirely of leftovers.

In terms of innovation and artistry *My Neighbours the Yamadas* is in a league of its own, certainly with regard to animated feature films. It is by turns anarchic and elegant, delicate and deranged, lowbrow and highbrow. As an experiment it was a bold move and one that did not set the box office alight – it was probably too revolutionary while at the same time appearing superficially naïve. It did, however, mark Ghibli's first entirely computer-generated feature, where the images were drawn using computers, albeit one as far away in look and feel as can be imagined from the likes of Pixar's perfectly rendered worlds. In 2003 Takahata contributed a segment to the collaborative animation *Winter Days*, similarly illustrating the works of Bashō but in a more contemplative yet scattershot fashion, recalling the manga of Hokusai in a succinct (one minute) experimental painting come to life. The sound of the cuckoo that announces Takahata's artist's relief at his successful bowel movement is similar to the visual and aural indicator that separates segments of *My Neighbours the Yamadas*.

Spirited Away (Sen to Chihiro no kamikakushi) (2001)

Written and directed by: Miyazaki Hayao

Chihiro is moving house, her past life withering away like the bouquet of flowers given to her by her friends. At least she *would* be moving if her parents had any sense of direction, careening their 4 x 4 through the countryside in search of clues as to where on earth they actually are. Coming to a dead end, they decide to find their bearings, taking a tunnel to what appears to be a disused theme park. Although the place seems deserted, Chihiro's hungry parents smell food. Delicious food. They tuck into a mound of goodies like beasts possessed as Chihiro looks on in shock. Leaving them to their gorging she comes across Haku, a handsome boy who warns her that she must leave before nightfall. Too late. Chihiro returns to her gluttonous folks to find them transformed into obese swine. All is not well in wonderland; it is a cruel and frightening place filled with spirits and supernatural creatures all overseen by the cackling sorceress Yubāba, a haggard, dumpy dictator. Unfortunately for Chihiro it is a world that does not allow humans; in order to survive and rescue her parents, currently indistinguishable from any of the other pigs being fattened for slaughter, she needs to find employment, a task that proves unpleasant and difficult. Retained by Yubāba she is renamed Sen and set to do the world's most disgusting jobs in the bathhouse. She has to bide her time and think of a plan. But even with Haku's help she slowly loses sight of her identity and her mission, sucked into an unseen world that coexists with our own.

Hyperbole aside, *Spirited Away* was huge. Smashing the box-office record set by James Cameron's all-conquering *Titanic* it became Japan's highest-grossing film until surpassed by *Demon Slayer the Movie: Mugen Train* in 2020. Internationally, partly due to a distribution deal with Disney's Buena Vista, the film cemented Ghibli's position in the consciousness of the mainstream filmgoer. For many, this was their first exposure to anime. *Spirited Away* clearly wasn't Disney-cute, though. Its sense of menace is palpable and it was responsible for frightening many a child who sympathised with Chihiro's terrifying predicament. Financially the film was a monster, smashing the $200-million barrier before being seen outside of Japan. Its critical reception was equally favourable – scooping the internationally prestigious Golden Bear at the Berlin Film Festival as well as an Oscar for Best Animated Feature. This success is entirely justified – it is a masterpiece of cinema – but perhaps a little surprising for, outside its fantastical flights of wonder, *Spirited Away* is, at heart, a melancholy film.

Chihiro is a do-er, capable and intelligent, she is independent in spirit but does not shun responsibility. Her ability to adapt and be accepted into any social group is shown not only by the fact that she can survive in an otherworldly society but also by the gift of flowers from her old classmates. Her real problems lie with her parents. Miyazaki paints a stark contrast with the parenting in *My Neighbour Totoro*. Mei's father accepts his daughter's view of the world and creatures that he cannot see; he is supportive and attentive. Chihiro's greedy parents virtually ignore their daughter; they are self-centred and individualistic, driving an unnecessarily large, polluting car and, while acknowledging the existence of Shintō shrines, do little to pay their respects. Crucially, by the film's close they have not learned the error of their ways; amnesia about their ordeal means that Chihiro's future life is no different from when she started the adventure. If *My Neighbour Totoro* is a nostalgic look at the past, *Spirited Away* is a lament for it from the perspective of the present. But there is hope. Although her parents' generation has let her down, Chihiro nevertheless has the spirit, the *ki*, to restore these fading values. The future lies in the hands of the children. Indeed, *Spirited Away* is very much a film about childhood and growing up, about responsibilities and the threats of the world. Miyazaki approaches this in a fantastical and spiritual manner but the message that childhood isn't easy is clear – Ghibli films never mollycoddle their audiences, even in the feel-good realms of *My Neighbour Totoro* and *Kiki's Delivery Service*. Rather, his child characters are put into situations of genuine peril with no guarantee of a positive outcome. Here, again, Miyazaki paints the world as seen by a youngster – a point of view that is anything but childish. The wonders that Chihiro faces are met from a child's perspective and she accepts what she sees at face value. In this way she learns what is safe and what is dangerous, not relying on preconceived ideas but adapting to circumstances. Not all that is monstrous to the eye is bad. In *Spirited Away* Chihiro faces a number of possible fates, none of them desirable. At a basic level, her discovery could lead to execution but, even worse, metaphysically, she could lose her identity. Yubāba, the huge-headed sorceress, maintains her power by taking people's names. Chihiro is renamed when Yubāba snatches the *kanji* (characters) of the name 'Ogino Chihiro' and discards all but one, leaving only a solitary *kanji* now pronounced 'Sen'. Yubāba's possession of her name means that Chihiro's identity will fade and her soul drift away.

The bewildering array of creatures featured in the film shows the diverse range of gods and spirits that populate Japanese mythology. Chihiro survives precisely because she understands the basics of the spirit world and quickly adapts to living within it. Almost all the residents have multiple forms and shapes. The outwardly human Haku, himself under the spell of Yubāba, is capable of transforming into a dragon. Yubāba is also capable of flight, turning into a monstrous bird. Kaonashi (No Face), the semi-transparent masked spirit that communicates with Chihiro through grunts and whimpers, is capable of becoming a ravenous monster who punishes the bathhouse residents greedy for gold. In this way, this world is a grotesque version of our own where greed and ambition mix with kindness and camaraderie.

The difference lies in extent and consequence. The results are dazzling and dizzying in their inventiveness: Kaonashi standing before Chihiro like a creature from Francis Bacon's *Three Studies for Figures at the Base of a Crucifixion* or the oversized Bō (sonny boy), a gargantuan baby whose wailings seem to be the only thing that can control Yubāba. Even the minor denizens are filled with character – the various frogs that work at the bathhouse or the *ootori-sama* (yellow, chick-like bird-gods) – as well as the more outlandish bit players – *ushioni* (wide-eyed demons with colourful hair and antlers who wear traditional dress) and *oshira-sama* (the bulbous *daikon* [radish] god that Chihiro squeezes into a lift with) among many others.

In terms of animation style, *Spirited Away* shows the confidence of a master who has honed his abilities but is capable of adopting new techniques when necessary. Some of the more elaborate shots in *Spirited Away* do use CGI, but normally this is restricted to putting hand-painted textures on simple geometric shapes to allow for 3-D tracking and also a number of shots that required steam and smoke effects. But they also used traditional techniques. Everything from the simple yet expressive *susuwatari* (soot sprites) to the elaborate and initially revolting Stink God is crafted to perfection. Miyazaki had come out of retirement in order to make *Spirited Away*, promptly declaring the film, on completion, to be his last. Until *Howl's Moving Castle*...

Like *My Neighbour Totoro*, *Spirited Away* also made the transition to the theatre. Toho Studios produced the live-action adaptation, which was directed by John Caird. It opened in Tōkyō in 2022 and ran for several months before touring various Japanese cities. Its European premiere will open in London in 2024.

The Cat Returns (Neko no ongaeshi) (2002)

Directed by: Morita Hiroyuki

'If you find yourself troubled by something mysterious or a problem that's hard to solve, there's a place you can go, a place where...'

Schoolgirl Yoshioka Haru is troubled by insurmountable problems, such as schoolwork and boys. Little does she know that these are soon to be the least of her worries. A curious thing happens when she spies a sleek grey cat trotting down the busy street, carrying in its mouth a carefully wrapped box topped with a red bow. The creature clearly has scant understanding of traffic laws, crossing the road into the path of a speeding van and narrowly avoiding a swift demise thanks to Haru's split-second decision to rescue it at the risk of her own life. To thank her the cat gracefully stands on its hind legs and bows, saying that he will show his gratitude at a later date. It turns out that the cat she has rescued is none other than Prince Lune, son of the King of the Kingdom of Cats who thanks her personally in a public parade. Soon her garden is full of feline-friendly foliage, she's covered in catnip and gifts of live mice are deposited in her school locker. Realising the interspecies *faux pas* they have caused, the cat world rethinks its remuneration package and the King comes up with an ideal solution – Haru should marry Prince Lune. Mortified at the idea of marrying a cat but intrigued by the thought of a luxurious life free of the pressures of the human world, Haru finds help in the unlikely trio of grumpy fat cat Muta, debonair Baron Humbert von Jikkingen and gargoyle-turned-crow Toto. She is kidnapped and taken to the Kingdom of Cats, her three companions in hot pursuit. Despite her objections, the King is adamant that the wedding ceremony will go ahead.

If Haru does not get back to the human world by dawn her transformation into a cat will be complete and irreversible. She already sports a tail and has sprouted a fine set of whiskers...

The nearest thing to a feature-length sequel that Studio Ghibli has produced, *The Cat Returns* is a companion piece to the delightful coming-of-age drama *Whisper of the Heart*. That film was about how normal life can be embellished by creating imaginary fantasy worlds, while *The Cat Returns* is more about these fantasies invading the real world – the flip side to the original. The first film had been a consistent favourite among Ghibli fans, who were drawn in particular to the enigmatic figure of Baron Humbert von Jikkingen. He plays a central role in the proceedings, but is shorn of any romantic interest and has become a gentleman adventurer. The genesis of the film was slightly unconventional in that it was originally intended to be a short film shown at a Japanese theme park. By the time that venture had fallen through, Ghibli had commissioned Hiiragi Aoi to return to Shizuku's world in manga form as a springboard for the project and had begun animation tests. Eager to nurture new talent Miyazaki gave the director's role to Morita Hiroyuki, a key animator on *My Neighbours the Yamadas*, who set about adapting Hiiragi's work into a longer form than originally intended. The film was released in Japanese cinemas in 2002. Partly due to its compact length, but also because Ghibli had often bundled films together for theatrical release, *The Cat Returns* ran as a double bill with the short *Ghiblies 2*.

The Cat Returns (the literal title is more like *The Cats' Requital*) is a frequently hilarious and inventive fantasy, a light and frothy film that never threatens to outgrow its running time of less than 80 minutes. However, it lacks much of the subtlety and thematic weight underpinning Ghibli's more lauded productions. Despite its flights of fancy, the film nevertheless has a strong sense of coherence because of how the characters interact with each other, particularly in the way that Haru saves not only Lune but also Lune's true love, Yuki. Yuki, now a beautiful white cat with a red collar, had been rescued by a young Haru who fed the bedraggled kitten with fish biscuits; now Yuki returns the favour by guiding Haru away from her escalating predicament. The fact that Lune is carrying a box of these very fish snacks for Yuki when Haru saves him from certain death further ties the story together.

The Baron from *Whisper of the Heart* is now revealed to be the official at the Cat Business Office, which Haru reaches by following Muta (Moon from *Whisper of the Heart*) into a previously unseen miniature European plaza. Muta is grumpy but is at heart a good cat, even though we later find out about his notoriety in the Kingdom of Cats as Renaldo Moon, a daring thief and a gourmet of little discrimination. (His gluttony proves to be his temporary downfall when he becomes encased in a bowl of catnip jelly.) The Baron, meanwhile, remains aloof from his companions' earthly vices. He invites Haru inside his office for a cup of his special-blend tea, but because of her *Alice in Wonderland* problem of scale she has to crawl through the doorway and cannot safely sit on the sofa. The Baron explains, 'This place is in a dimension a little different from yours, a world for beings who have souls. When people create something with all their hearts and hopes, the creation is given a soul.'

The Cat Returns concerns itself with these two things – dimensions and creativity. Unlike *Whisper of the Heart*, however, the creative side is realised explicitly on the screen rather than the film being about the creative process itself. These ideas are revealed in the various worlds that the film sketches out – creativity comes from these different dimensions, away from the constraints of the real world around us. Like infinite quantum universes, the realms of the imagination mean that new worlds, impossible worlds, can be created. The Baron's residence is in one such world. Haru faces the possibility of life in a soulless land if she gives in to apathy and joins the Kingdom of Cats. As the Baron advises, 'You must learn to be yourself.' Haru's struggle to be creative is seen in the ways in which she succumbs to the advantages of living in the Kingdom of Cats, realising early on that perhaps the life of a cat could be desirable – do nothing, eat lots and sleep. Indeed, as soon as she arrives in the Kingdom her first action is to lie spread-eagled in the grass, gazing lazily at the sky in utter contentment. The consequences become apparent, though, when she is told to change into a more appropriate dress. The beautiful pastel, yellow-and-white affair, complete with enchanting fish-design necklace, sees the first of her transformations into becoming a cat – her ears and nose turn feline. 'Neko!' she screams on seeing her metamorphosed reflection in the mirror. The true consequences of her (in) actions are externalised, her fate anything but secure when, at a banquet, she realises the extent of the King's power. Performers who fail to entertain him are hurled from the top of the castle battlements to a squishy fate.

Although the animation in *The Cat Returns* is slightly more simplified than other Ghibli films, the design is exemplary with an abundance of fanciful ideas. Individual sequences are among Ghibli's most memorable and enjoyable, although, as a whole, the film represents a minor work for the studio.

Howl's Moving Castle (Hauru no ugoku shiro) (2004)

Written (screenplay) and directed by: Miyazaki Hayao

Howl, a ladies' man and wizard, roams the country with apparent impunity, his smoke-belching, moving castle stomping across the landscape without a care. But is he really so brazenly free? In some quarters he travels incognito, trading under names like Pendragon or Jenkins. And how can such a flamboyant wizard survive in such turbulent times? The world is on the brink of war and the King is mustering all the wizards and witches he can to gain advantage over his enemies. Worse still, the notorious Witch of the Waste is rumoured to be abroad, spreading her vile canker with evil subterfuge. A matter for the great and mighty, you might think, but the ramifications affect even the apparently insignificant. Young milliner Sophie becomes embroiled in this web of intrigue when she is saved by Howl from the uncouth attentions of a pair of boisterous soldiers. Matters take a turn for the worse when the Witch of the Waste visits her shop and curses her, transforming the girl into an old woman who is unable to reveal the cause of her sorry fate. Sophie flees her hometown and pursues Howl's moving castle, gaining access to the elusive ramshackle abode with the aid of a perpetually grinning, turnip-headed scarecrow. There she meets Calcifer, a fire-demon with an unspecified bond to the castle's owner, and Markl, a boy wizard. Sophie sets about cleaning the castle, not always with the approval of its residents, but such acts of domesticity soon pale into insignificance as tensions between the nations escalate.

Miyazaki's intention to retire was once more put on hold when he decided to film *Howl's Moving Castle*, an adaptation of the book by Diana Wynne Jones. Originally, Hosoda Mamoru (animator and director of *The Girl Who Leapt through Time* [2006], *Summer Wars* [2009], *Wolf Children* [2012] and *Belle* [2021]) was expected to direct the project, but he pulled out, leaving Miyazaki to take the reins and adapt the screenplay, which was more in tune with his own vision. It's easy to see why the idea appealed to him because the castle itself is clearly a designer's dream. Coupled with this are common Miyazaki themes about identity and humanity but, importantly, as with *Laputa: Castle in the Sky*, reaction to real-world events shaped the story and pushed it in a different direction from the source novel. However, Jones liked the finished result very much, 'I was overwhelmed, actually... It was rich and strange and full of the most beautiful animation.'

As with Chihiro in *Spirited Away*, Sophie faces an identity crisis – what separates the two characters is that, in *Howl's Moving Castle*, this crisis is a physical rather than spiritual one. Sophie has been transformed into an old woman by the Witch of the Waste and takes on her role with stoic reluctance. It impacts on her physical appearance but basically reflects what Sophie feels about herself – castigating her own looks. Paradoxically, when there is no chance of retaining her former features due to her ancient appearance, she becomes more free and confident in herself, able to tackle tasks with aplomb because she has nothing to lose. This contrasts with the narcissistic Howl, a man so beholden to his own image that the thought of losing his absurdly handsome, androgynous looks is enough to send him into a life-threatening bout of depression – 'What's the point of living if you can't be beautiful?' These sulky episodes are compounded by Howl's basic loss of his humanity, the result of a pact that has rendered him at once powerful but also vulnerable, hiding behind disguises in an attempt to shirk responsibility or avoid confronting the Witch of the Waste. When he does attempt to do good and face the enemy in the terrible war, the cost to his humanity is greater still for, after transforming into a giant black bird, it becomes increasingly difficult for him to revert back to human form. What grasp he has on his soul is slipping away. The war in this film is politically motivated and has parallels with the US-led invasion of Iraq. The deeds of powerful men have ramifications for everyone and no one is free from the burden of choice in adversity. Miyazaki was interviewed in US magazine *Newsweek* in June 2005 and made his views on the issue clear: 'Actually, your country had just started the war against Iraq, and I had a great deal of rage about that. So I felt some hesitation about the award [Academy Award for *Spirited Away*]. In fact, I had just started to make *Howl's Moving Castle*, so the film is profoundly affected by the war in Iraq.'

Sophie's freedom from being self-conscious about her image – 'You're still healthy and those clothes finally suit you,' as she says to her reflection in the mirror – and her removal from her restrictive home life have given her a huge sense of compassion. When the Witch of the Waste is stripped of her powers and reduced to a dotty, selfish old woman, it is Sophie, still under her curse, who takes pity and looks after her. Similarly, although she views him with some suspicion, Sophie allows the King's sorceress Suliman's dog and spy to accompany them. Through these acts of kindness Sophie shows that benevolence can change people more than war and subjugation. It just takes time.

Howl's Moving Castle is filled with images that are by turns delightful and frightening. The Victorian-style, steam-driven cities, with their trains and mechanical cars, are supplemented by astounding flying vehicles – belching, screeching animals of death. Huge battleships limp into port following defeat at sea and the skies are buzzing with the drone of war. Prowling the streets in the build-up to conflict are lecherous soldiers and blob men, sinister, dark shapes that ooze from the walls and do the nefarious bidding of their mistress, the Witch of the Waste, a malformed old woman with too much make-up who sweats spite from her rancid pores. Contrasting with this malice is Turnip (*Kabu*), the mute, bouncing scarecrow who helps out around (but not in) the castle by hanging out the washing. Holding the castle together is chirpy fire-demon Calcifer, bound to Howl by a powerful magical force so that their fates, and that of the castle, are irrevocably intertwined. Completing the misfit family – for *Howl's Moving Castle* is a film that advocates finding your own family rather than relying on the one you are born into – is Markl, a wizard in training.

A major theme in *Howl's Moving Castle* is that of change or metamorphosis, either through magic or nature – a regular feature of Miyazaki's films. From the subtle oncoming of puberty in *Kiki's Delivery Service*, through Marco's transformation in *Porco Rosso*, the multiple metamorphoses in *Spirited Away* to the various iterations of characters in *The Boy and the Heron*, change marks the passage of time, the pollution of the spirit or an alteration of the balance between humanity and the void. Nowhere is this more apparent than in *Howl's Moving Castle* where Sophie is turned into an old woman magically, but it is implied that, spiritually, her low self-esteem is just as much to blame for her condition. Sparkles of her youth return when asleep, when she displays confidence or when Howl takes her to his 'secret garden'. The Witch of the Waste similarly changes; when drained of her powers her whole physical appearance alters. Markl, Howl's apprentice, casually dons a beard to look older while Howl himself is locked in a struggle for his soul, made manifest in the increasing difficulty he finds changing back from bird to man. Howl's world is one in which people, as a result of traps or curses, are turned into something they are not, often for political purposes. Even someone as powerful as Howl finds it difficult to stand up to the establishment in his struggle to aid a people subjugated by the propaganda of terror.

Once again there is use of CGI amidst the predominantly cel animation – up to 200 shots incorporated digital imagery but many were retouched to achieve a consistency with the hand-drawn images. The most extensive use of CGI is with the castle itself, but the effect is subtle; it looks more like an intricate animation by Terry Gilliam than a computer-generated picture. After *Howl's Moving Castle*, Miyazaki moved back to more traditional forms of animation with the short films for the Studio Ghibli Museum, 10- to 20-minute experiments, and *Ponyo on the Cliff by the Sea*, a film made entirely by hand.

Tales from Earthsea (Gedo senki) (2006)

Directed by: Miyazaki Gorō

'Long ago dragons and men were one.'

Prince Arren returns to court after a brief absence, kills his father and steals the monarch's still-sheathed sword before fleeing. The land is in disarray, the Light of the Balance is getting weaker, dragons are fighting to the death and the result is pestilence and desolation. The citizens are seeking release from real-world misery by imbibing the highly addictive *hazia*. Arren finds a trusted companion in the shape of Sparrowhawk (Gedo), who saves him from a pack of wolves. 'I doubt our meeting here was an accident,' he tells Arren. They travel to the city and Sparrowhawk rescues him again after Arren saves a girl, Therru, from the unwanted attentions of ruthless slavers but is captured himself. Together they form an unlikely family at Sparrowhawk's trusted friend and confidant Tenar's farm outside the city. But Lord Cob, an evil wizard who is responsible for the slave trade, has spies abroad and nowhere is safe. Arren becomes increasingly restless when he sees a shadow copy of himself roaming the landscape. Meanwhile, Lord Cob's men invade the farm and capture Tenar, while the wizard himself, having a score to settle with Sparrowhawk, finds Arren and sets about trying to manipulate him into revealing his true name.

Ursula K Le Guin's ground-breaking fantasy novels for young adults, with their dragons and heroes, seem ideally suited to Ghibli's oeuvre. For many years Miyazaki Hayao had been interested in adapting the books, but a combination of work commitments and rights issues (indeed, the release of *Tales from Earthsea* in the US was delayed because it clashed with a live adaptation that effectively ruled out its showing for at least three years) meant that he never had the opportunity. Eventually Ghibli obtained the rights to the book in 2003 but, in what was seen by many as a strange choice, the film was handed to a first-time director – Miyazaki Gorō, Hayao's son. Miyazaki Gorō, who worked in landscaping, had been designing the Ghibli Museum when he was approached to come up with some storyboard ideas for the film by producer Suzuki Toshio. Miyazaki Hayao was still busy finishing *Howl's Moving Castle* and so, impressed with what he saw, Suzuki gave the job of directing *Tales from Earthsea* to Miyazaki Gorō. It was a daunting baptism of fire but one supported by the team of expert animators at the studio, including animation director Inamura Takeshi, who had worked for Ghibli for many years.

Tales from Earthsea is a sweeping film that seeks to adapt not just *A Wizard of Earthsea* (the source for the doppelganger subplot, although it doesn't apply to Arren but to Gedo/Sparrowhawk in the book) but all four of the *Earthsea* books: *The Tombs of Atuan* (Tenar's backstory), *The Farthest Shore* (which covers most of the plot) and *Tehanu* (Therru's story). *Tales from Earthsea* intertwines the various plot strands so that events happen concurrently. For example, the revelation that if a wizard knows someone's true name it gives them power over that person and the draining of magical power in the land are themes that mirror the first and third books in the series. The style is reminiscent of *Shuna's Journey* (1983), a manga that Miyazaki Hayao had created before beginning *Nausicaä*. The character design of Therru, the residents and town of Hort, as well as Tenar's farm and Sparrowhawk's steed all bear a resemblance to that graphic novel.

Thematically, *Tales from Earthsea* touches on many of the issues that are common in other Studio Ghibli films. The concern for the environment, while not so explicit, features in the way that dwindling magic has affected crops and people's livelihoods. More overt are the ideas about identity and change. In *Spirited Away* Chihiro/Sen has her name, which is her essence, taken from her by Yubāba, and when she loses that she loses everything. In *Tales from Earthsea*, Arren is tricked by Lord Cob into revealing his true name, Lebannen, and the wizard uses the name to exert power over the boy. 'Magic is the power to command if you know a thing's true name,' as Sparrowhawk had explained to Arren. This duality of personalities and the process of metamorphosis can be seen in the more powerful characters that hold the film together, from Arren's other self to the dragons that battle at the film's opening and closing – potent wizards in different forms. These dragons are immense and impressive. Sparrowhawk also metamorphoses in order to gain reconnaissance information or move swiftly from one place to another. Lord Cob uses his magic to transform himself at many key points in the film, especially at the denouement when his guise as an oozing black angel of death becomes one of the film's key extended set pieces. The use of animation here is spectacular as Cob transforms himself into a flying blob of hate, his eyes long since retracted into his face to show cold, empty sockets.

Where the film finds its voice is in the details, particularly those that relate to characterisation. What's interesting is how minor characters possess succinctly fleshed-out traits that make them rounded and believable. When two old women go to Tenar's farm they want to procure a potion from the benevolent witch but make no bones about the fact that they view her with suspicion and derision. Their hypocrisy in accepting Tenar's help is confirmed when they have no hesitation about giving up the witch's location to Cob's thugs for a couple of coins (which they don't actually receive).

Tales from Earthsea's combination of fantasy, magic, dragons and quests is an enticing one. Unfortunately, the simple plot (two rival wizards) mixed with complex subplots (taking in four novels) makes for uneven viewing. The problem is compounded by a lack of context for the main characters, particularly Arren, who we first see killing his father; subsequently, it's difficult for the audience to identify with him as a hero. Nevertheless, the film is engaging. Particularly noteworthy are the backdrop paintings that at times seem to glow from the screen, and the exemplary architectural designs.

Of some interest is Miyazaki Gorō's choice of casting for the film. Okada Junichi, a member of the boy band V6, plays Arren and singer Teshima Aoi voices Therru (she also sings 'Therru's Song' which closes the film). Most interesting is the casting of Sugawara Bunta as Sparrowhawk/Gedo. He had worked for Ghibli before on *Spirited Away* but is best known for a series of hard-hitting *yakuza* (gangster) films made with maverick director Fukasaku Kinji. These cast members add an air of importance to the film that is sadly lacking in the lacklustre English-language version.

Tales from Earthsea opened to a predictably large box office, remaining the number-one film in Japan for many weeks. There were, however, rumblings of discontent about the film – with *Shūkan Bunshun* magazine awarding it 'Worst Film' in their annual poll of critics and Miyazaki Gorō picking up 'Worst Director'. Ursula K Le Guin, too, was disappointed with some elements of the film. In many ways this reaction was inevitable. Miyazaki Gorō had to live up to Ghibli's unassailable hold on the public consciousness. If he had rigorously adapted the book or closely imitated his father's style, people would have complained about a lack of imagination. If he had diverged further from the book and experimented more with the style, people would have accused him of folly or hubris. In the end they did both. *Tales from Earthsea* is an ambitious film that has moments that border on brilliance but does suffer from fluctuating pacing. For any other animation studio *Tales from Earthsea* would be a jewel in their crown and such quibbles ignored. Just not for Studio Ghibli.

Ponyo on the Cliff by the Sea (Gake no ue no Ponyo) (2008)

Written and directed by: Miyazaki Hayao

> *'I made this movie with the intent that five-year-old children would be able to understand it, even if 50-year-olds can't.'*

Sōsuke lives on a cliff overlooking the sea in a charming little house with his mother Lisa. His father Kōichi works on a ship so is often absent from their lives for long stretches of time. One day Sōsuke finds a strange creature stuck in a jar, a fishlike being with a human's head that he names Ponyo. Ponyo has escaped from the submarine laboratory of her father Fujimoto in an attempt to gain freedom. Sōsuke keeps Ponyo in a green bucket of water that he hides in the bushes whenever he attends the school adjacent to the old people's home where Lisa works. Ponyo and Sōsuke enjoy each other's company but Fujimoto seeks to get his errant daughter back, dispatching ominous dark aqua fish to snatch her and return her to his submarine. But Ponyo is slowly falling in love with Sōsuke and desires to be human, using magic to sprout birdlike limbs that eventually evolve into arms and legs. She escapes Fujimoto's clutches once more to be reunited with Sōsuke. Meanwhile the unfettered use of magic seems to be affecting the natural balance of the world.

Although the films of Miyazaki do have a broad appeal there is a sense that *Ponyo on the Cliff by the Sea* is a return to more child-friendly pictures like *My Neighbour Totoro* and *Kiki's Delivery Service* rather than the more visceral *Princess Mononoke* or the downright terrifying *Spirited Away*. On the surface *Ponyo* has an uncluttered and neatly defined visual style that is elegant and fresh, but, in many ways, this is one of Miyazaki's most ambitious projects. In order to realise this aesthetic Miyazaki turned his back on CGI entirely, relying instead on traditional means of animating the film. The result was that about 170,000 animation cels were used in the production – a staggering amount that surpassed the numbers used on his previous films. The results of this incredible labour are apparent on the screen in the organic way the waves lash on the shoreline or in the incredible opening sequences set beneath the sea where schools of jellyfish undulate in the underwater turbulence. The sea itself becomes a central character in the film, lashing out or rolling gently in as expressive a way as any of the humans or creatures. The effect is that the animation feels right – it feels alive and organic. Miyazaki's desire to make a film that would appeal to and be understood by someone the same age as his five-year-old hero is evident not only in the fantastical story but in this simple and naturalistic style. The key to Miyazaki's brand of fantasy lies in bringing the magical, the spiritual and the fantastical into very real and detailed worlds. His films are so believable and involving precisely because the juxtaposition of the natural and the fantastical is so cleverly realised. In *Ponyo* we instantly accept the strange little fishlike creature with her mop of ginger hair and expressive eyes, precisely because she is animated in as realistic a way as the earlier jellyfish. As with the Ohmu in *Nausicaä of the Valley of the Wind* or the *kodama* in *Princess Mononoke*, it is the sheer number of independently animated bodies – here an almost unprecedented number – which enhance the believability of the scene. Although such scenes of massive swarms of computer-generated animals have become commonplace in the cinema with the use of dynamic simulations, the hand-animated schools of fish give each creature true individuality. The non-fantastical creatures are portrayed so accurately that you wonder whether the Ghibli Museum shorts *Looking for a Home* and particularly *Water Spider Monmon* were used as a testing ground to see if aquatic life could be animated convincingly. Both films were finished in 2006, just as Miyazaki was starting work on *Ponyo*.

As with many of Miyazaki's films, *Ponyo on the Cliff by the Sea* is inspired by a distinct geographical location, like the Sayama Forest of *My Neighbour Totoro*, Yakushima's forests in *Princess Mononoke*, or the area around the Ghibli studio in *Koro's Big Stroll* (2001). Indeed Ghibli publications relating to *Koro* and *Ponyo* provide handy maps of the locations used. In the case of *Ponyo*, the film is set around the port town of Tomonoura, which Miyazaki had visited in 2004. It's a popular tourist destination among Japanese people with a large, island-based hotel for visitors. Like much of coastal Japan (the largely mountainous centre of the country means that the majority of people live near the sea), the area is always potentially at risk from tsunami, an event shown in *Ponyo* to have been generated by an unbalancing of the Earth's magic.

Once again Joe Hisaishi provides the score, but this time the music is far more diverse than in previous Miyazaki films and takes in a number of sources and styles that are very sophisticated, particularly for a film aimed at children. Most memorable, however, is the film's closing theme song, an infectious number sung by eight-year-old Ohashi Nozomi, which was cheerfully mimicked by the hordes of Japanese children enamoured by the film. Elsewhere the score is more traditionally orchestral, occasionally recalling Wagner's epic *Der Ring des Nibelungen* (*The Ring of the Nibelung*) cycle. This is not as strange as it may at first appear since there are some links to *The Ring* in the narrative – on Ponyo's recapture Fujimoto refers to her as Brünnhilde, which is the name of Wotan's top Valkyrie (and, in Wagner's epic, one of Wotan's many daughters), who betrays her father. This in turn leads to another common theme among Miyazaki heroines, that of identity and loss. Like in *Spirited Away*, the heroine's identity is inexorably linked to her name and who she wants to be. Having decided on love and humanity, Ponyo resolutely sticks with her adopted, human, name.

The balance between fantasy and reality is reflected in *Ponyo* in the way that the environment is affected by the delicate balances in both the natural world and the magical one. Ponyo's initial escape from Fujimoto almost turns into a disaster as she tries to negotiate the polluted, litter-strewn ocean bed, struggling free of a trawler's dragnet but finding herself trapped inside a discarded jar. Once again humans threaten their surroundings but there is a sense that the fantastical beings – including Ponyo's father and mother – also have a responsibility to maintain the environmental balance. When Ponyo decides that she wishes to become human, her transformation upsets the balance of the world. It causes the tsunami that helps reunite her with Sōsuke but also results in massive destruction and the forced evacuation of the town. Ponyo must make amends for this.

The relationships in *Ponyo* are a realistic depiction of a happy and stable family unit. As with *My Neighbour Totoro*, one of the parents is absent but this is a result of his work. While this creates tension between Lisa and her husband, the frustration is born out of a desire for the family to be together, not because of breakdown. Despite her annoyance at his failure to return home, communicated in an angry but amusing burst of insults on an Aldis lamp, Lisa is another of Miyazaki's resourceful working women – she looks after her son but also works hard at the old people's home. She is more than capable of holding her own and, in the film's electrifying, rain-drenched car chase, drives so aggressively it would make Arsène Lupin blanch. Despite this, the film focuses more on the abilities of the old and the young to deal with the boundaries between the real and the fantastical; they are shown to be more open and able to accept that which is beyond everyday understanding. Indeed, Miyazaki's stated aim that 'five-year-old children will be able to understand it, even if 50-year-olds can't' is precisely the point of both his film and the way his characters act within it.

Ponyo is one of Miyazaki's most memorable characters in that she is both fantastical and real. She reacts to everything in an inquisitive manner, without fear, just as children growing up examine the world around them, oblivious of danger. She's also cheeky – spitting out jets of water with alarming accuracy to indicate anything from amusement to displeasure. Like a child she slowly learns the protocols of language and her relationship with Sōsuke changes from that of rescued pet to beloved companion.

Although there is tension and threat throughout *Ponyo* – the menacing aqua fish, dark waves with sinister eyes and the terrifying effects of the tsunami – the way it is handled makes the whole piece feel like an adventure. In *Spirited Away* the threat is palpable and sustained but *Ponyo on the Cliff by the Sea* tempers its moments of danger, which are exciting and invigorating, with periods of stability. To this end, rather like characters such as the Witch of the Waste in *Howl's Moving Castle*, there is always the possibility of redemption. *Ponyo* is a life-affirming film that sees the possibilities for good in everyone as well as accepting that all people, good or bad, are capable of causing mishaps, intentionally or not.

Ponyo on the Cliff by the Sea is another delightful addition to the Miyazaki canon, a freewheeling adventure about companionship with breathtaking animation and beautifully crafted key sequences. Many critics have made comparisons with *My Neighbour Totoro* but this is, if you'll excuse the pun, a different kettle of fish, eschewing the focused minimalism of the former film in favour of an almost stream-of-consciousness adventure that brings out the child in everyone.

Arrietty (The Borrower Arrietty, Kari-gurashi no Arietti) (2010)

Directed by: Yonebayashi Hiromasa

Twelve-year-old Shō is spending the summer at his mother's childhood home. It's an impressive house, but it isn't his holiday residence that will make his stay so unforgettable. You see, Arrietty and her parents also live in the same abode; from a race of tiny people, they survive by 'borrowing' objects that won't be missed from the household. One evening Arrietty is taken on her first borrowing excursion with her father, Pod. Their aim is to procure a sugar lump and a tissue. She discovers the most wonderful doll's house in Shō's bedroom but is warned not to borrow anything from it, lest the 'human beans' discover anything missing. Their borrowing mission is not a success when Arrietty is spotted by Shō. She drops the sugar lump. The next morning he leaves it, along with a note, outside the air vent which the Borrowers use to access the garden. Feisty Arrietty climbs to Shō's room to return the sugar lump and request that the boy leave them alone. Pod and his wife, Homily, realise that Arrietty has been in contact with humans, so decide that they are no longer safe and should relocate elsewhere. When Pod returns injured from a borrowing expedition, he is assisted by Spiller, another of their kind, who advises that there are alternative places to stay. Shō wants to help the little people, and replaces Homily's kitchen under the floor with that from the doll's house. Arrietty meets with Shō and tells him they will have to leave. The young man reveals that he has a heart condition. Meanwhile, housekeeper, Haru, discovers the kitchen furniture missing from the doll's house and eventually finds Homily, confirming her long-held suspicion that little people, in fact, not only live in the house, but also steal items from it. She grabs the terrified Homily, drops her into a glass jar, locks Shō in his room and calls the pest control company. Shō manages to escape and helps Arrriety rescue her mother, then removes all traces of their presence. Haru believes them to be thieves but Shō recognises, 'They're not thieves at all! They're Borrowers.' As the Borrower family depart, the cat leads Shō to the river, where he finds them about to embark on their journey inside a kettle. He brings Arrietty a sugar lump and bids her farewell, telling her that her courage has given him the confidence to undergo his operation and to live.

Mary Norton's novel *The Borrowers* was first published in 1952 and led to many additional books in the series, becoming a favourite in children's literature. Its popularity led to a number of adaptations, from movies to TV series. Reminiscent of anime adaptations of other classic literature, such as those produced for the *World Masterpiece Theater* series that Miyazaki and Takahata worked on during the 1970s, it is easy to see how Ghibli would have been interested in adapting *The Borrowers*. Indeed they had been considering an adaptation for many decades. Miyazaki noted, 'There's something Takahata and I used to talk about in our 20s... There were many adaptations of famous stories, but they rejected works that were totally original. They thought there'd be no audience and that animation was for children. That's why the story had to be familiar to parents, so the parents would give permission for their children to see the films.' The story's appeal to the animators is clear: it's a fantasy that is set in an ordinary home with central characters whose lives are necessarily secretive. This kind of link between the fantastical and the ordinary world can be seen in many Ghibli films, from the tunnel that leads to the spiritual world in *Spirited Away* to the premise that Totoro is living next door to Mei and Satsuki.

Arrietty is a reasonably faithful adaptation of the first book in the series; it makes alterations to certain events and a significant change is the introduction of Spiller, who doesn't appear in the first novel but joins the family in the second book, *The Borrowers Afield* (1955). Crucially, unlike *Tales from Earthsea*, the film doesn't try to merge a number of stories and this ensures that the final product has a simple and concise narrative. The most significant alteration is that of the setting; *Arrietty* is set in a Japanese household rather than a grand old English country house. Despite many Ghibli films being set in European cities, it was decided that a familiar setting would appeal more to local viewers. 'The Japanese audience wouldn't come and see it if I hadn't changed it,' stated Miyazaki, who co-wrote the screenplay. This makes sense because, while a city's buildings may possess a variety of different architectural and decorative styles, they still retain familiarity as a city, whereas the interiors of

Japanese homes are different to those of Western homes. The mise-en-scène is important as we see how the animators have adapted Japanese-style living accommodation (sliding doors and cupboards) to suit the world of the Borrowers. However, some aspects of Western furniture and decor can be seen. Despite the alterations the setting remains true to the spirit of the book which states, in a bookending chapter that has been dropped from the film, 'If they exist at all, you would only find them in houses which are old and quiet and deep in the country – and where the human beings live to a routine.'

Social and environmental issues are discussed in both the film and the novel, as we learn during Arrietty's conversation with Shō that the Borrowers appear to be a 'doomed species', even verging on extinction. This would seem to be true. The only other Borrower who appears in the film is the somewhat uncommunicative, albeit helpful, Spiller, although he indicates that he is aware of others of their kind. Shō discusses how the environment has changed for many species, which has resulted in population decline. Even though she has considered this possibility herself Arrietty, rightly, feels insulted that Shō should imply that their kind is endangered, but Shō admits that he has a heart condition and is expecting to die. There is hope for a positive future for the family – as there so often is in Ghibli films – but they will have to work hard, to strive, wherever they locate to in order to ensure the safety and welfare of their little community. We know that Arrietty is determined to do this. 'We won't give up so easily,' she declares.

The book was adapted into a screenplay by Miyazaki (with Niwa Keiko) but was the directorial debut of Yonebayashi Hiromasa. Yonebayashi had worked as an animator at Studio Ghibli for a number of years, starting out as an in-betweener on *Princess Mononoke* and later going on to direct *When*

Marnie Was There. In his late 30s when he directed *Arrietty*, Yonebayashi was Ghibli's youngest director ever to take the helm. Although the studio has always tried to integrate and expand the skills of talented animators, Yonebayashi was, according to Miyazaki, a reluctant director. 'He wouldn't be the director otherwise, as he never wanted to be one.' The direction is solid and *Arrietty* is an easy film to watch; it has a linear narrative that is well constructed, with high-quality animation and exemplary character design. While *Arrietty* doesn't have the more extreme fantastical aspects of Miyazaki's works or the wonderful experimental edge of Takahata's films it remains a charming, if undemanding, fantasy.

From Up on Poppy Hill (Kokuriko-zaka kara) (2011)

Directed by: Miyazaki Gorō

'Destroy the old and you destroy the memory of our past.'

1963. Yokohama schoolgirl Matsuzaki Umi starts her daily routine at home, a boarding residence where she, her younger siblings, Sora and Riku, and opinionated grandmother, Hana, live, along with a number of paying guests. Umi's mother, Ryōko, is currently studying in America, so Umi takes on many of the boarding house's chores, particularly cooking meals. There is another task – a personal endeavour – that she sets herself daily. Every morning she raises shipping signal flags to broadcast a message from her hilltop home across to the sea for her father to see. Although her father died many years ago, this routine provides her with a link to him. She goes to school at the Konan Academy, where the student newspaper has published a gushing poem to her daily ritual. This newsletter, like many of the school's extracurricular activities, is generated in the Quartier

Latin, a decrepit old building that faces demolition at the behest of the school governors. Initially this is supported by the majority of the pupils, but newspaper editor Kazama Shun is determined that the old building be preserved and engages in a stunt which sees him jump from its roof into a pool in the playground. The clubhouse is the domain of the boys, from the philosophy to the chemistry to the astronomy clubs. Shun's stunt leads to Umi and Sora meeting with him, and he asks Umi if she would help with the production of the newspaper. She suggests that perhaps the female pupils might spend more time in the building if it was cleaned. She, and an army of classmates, male and female, undertake the task of cleaning and redecorating.

Umi and Shun develop a friendship and, on a visit to the boarding house, she shows him a photo of her father with two of his best friends. It turns out that Shun has an exact copy of this picture and asks his adoptive father to confirm who his real father was. It appears that, by a tragic twist of fate, Umi and Shun could be siblings. Shun tries to distance himself from Umi and they both admit that they have feelings for each other, but accept that they should simply remain friends. Umi's mother returns home and tries to help unravel the mystery. She reveals that Tachibana Hiroshi is Shun's father; Umi's father registered the child as his own to avoid him having to go to an orphanage, but because Ryōko was pregnant with Umi, they decided to give the child to Shun's adoptive parents. The pair take a trip to Tōkyō with their friend Shirō to convince Chairman Tokumaru that he shouldn't demolish the clubhouse. The jovial chairman agrees to visit them and is delighted to see the passion the pupils have for their activities. He decides to retain the building. The third person in the photo is Yoshio Onodera, captain of a ship currently located in the harbour, but about to leave on a long voyage. Shun and Umi receive a message that they should meet with him.

He reveals how their fathers were his best friends and confirms that the pair are not related and therefore able to commence the romance they so desire.

From Up on Poppy Hill is Miyazaki Gorō's second animation following *Tales from Earthsea*, which didn't fare well at the box office or receive critical acclaim. Rather than continue working in the fantasy genre, he decided to make a drama based in the real world, which tells the story of a burgeoning romance. Whereas Miyazaki Hayao had not been involved with *Earthsea*, for this film he developed the screenplay (with Niwa Keiko) from the 1980 manga written by Sayama Tetsurō and illustrated by Takahashi Chizuru. It's another coming-of-age drama, reminiscent of the other real-world Ghibli films such as (cat incidents aside) *Whisper of the Heart* and *Ocean Waves*. These are films which depict young protagonists, on the cusp of adulthood, where the possibility of romance may be determined not just by their respective situations but also by location and time, current or past events, and sometimes wider social contexts. To this end the primary difficulty that Umi and Shun face is a potential taboo – the possibility that they might be siblings – just one more addition to the emotional upheaval that many teenagers face. Unlike *Only Yesterday*, which follows two clearly defined timelines for the same protagonist, *From Up on Poppy Hill* uses flashbacks to show the story's different perspectives as the young couple try to determine their parentage, rather than using the protagonists' recollections of the past to reflect upon the present. Here past events are revealed through other people's memories because the central characters were too young when the incidents that affected their lives took place.

The film is set in 1963 and Miyazaki Gorō deliberately set out to make a period film, 'an idealised picture'. It captures the spirit of the Japanese people who, having suffered greatly during and immediately after World War Two, started the arduous task of rebuilding their country, a process that would eventually lead to Japan's 'economic miracle' of the 1980s. We see this spirit reflected in Umi's 'can-do' attitude to everything she takes on. She takes her responsibilities seriously – not only does she work hard at her studies, she also shops and cooks meals for the boarding house guests, deals with some of the financial aspects of running the guest house (thanks to additional funding from her grandmother), works on the school newspaper and completes her daily flag-flying ritual. *From Up on Poppy Hill* also directly acknowledges World War Two but in a very different way to the horror of the Kōbe bombings in *Grave of the Fireflies* or the creation of fighter aeroplanes in *The Wind Rises*. It discusses the confusion of civilian lives turned upside down by events beyond their control; how Umi and Shun's parents tried to do the right thing, to help their friends. It also refers to Japan's involvement with the Korean War, which was being fought by the Americans who had occupied Japan following World War Two. Although Japan was not strictly involved in the war, a number of vessels were used for military support duties. In the film, Umi's father's boat, a cargo ship, was destroyed by a mine. She clings to the memories of him, living her hopes from childhood by flying the flags daily to bid his return, a return that she knows cannot occur. Her elderly grandmother says, 'I hope you find someone wonderful soon, then you won't need the flags.'

Set at a time of great social change, the film acknowledges the past – the post-war chaos and confusion – while depicting a present that offers hope. The film references the forthcoming Tokyo Olympic Games, an event that was due to be held in that city in 1940 but was cancelled because of the war and had to wait until 1964. This event would give Japan the opportunity to showcase itself to the world. The students' determination to preserve their old clubhouse reflects the ethos seen in many Ghibli films – that of respect for the past while looking to the future. It is, perhaps, particularly pertinent that such an optimistic film was created during 2011. Following the devastating tsunami on 11 March and subsequent nuclear disaster at Fukushima, there were rolling blackouts due to the lack of power, and this meant that aspects of the production which required the use of computers moved onto a night-time schedule when there was less demand for energy.

Music compositions are integral to the film, with links to songs and tunes that represent the era of the film's setting as well as its story line, some of which were lyricised or adapted by Miyazaki Gorō himself. The film's main theme song was recorded the day before the 2011 earthquake. A number of group songs reflect community solidarity and make the film believable as something distinct in its portrayal of Japanese society, yet with sentiments that are universal. *From Up on Poppy Hill* addresses incest, war and grief but in an extremely engaging way, even if the lead protagonists themselves note that, 'It's like some cheap melodrama.'

From Up on Poppy Hill was the highest-grossing Japanese film of 2011 in its home country, taking over $56 million at the box office. It generally received good notices from critics and also won the Best Animation award at the Japan Academy Awards.

The Wind Rises (Kaze tachinu) (2013)

Written and directed by: Miyazaki Hayao

Young Horikoshi Jirō wishes to become a pilot, but his eyesight is too poor for him to realise his ambitions of flying aeroplanes. As he grows up Jirō pursues his dreams, visions which often comprise conversations with Italian aircraft designer Caproni. Aeronautical engineering beckons as a career and Horikoshi studies for his degree at Tōkyō University. While travelling on the train he meets a young girl, Naoko, who catches his hat when it flies away in the breeze. Disaster strikes later when the train is halted following a massive earthquake (the Great Kanto earthquake of 1923) and he assists the young girl's maid, who has broken her leg, creating a splint using his slide rule and taking them to their suburban home. He excels as a student. Following graduation, Horikoshi and his friend Honjō Kirō get jobs with Mitsubishi, their design work overseen by their boss, the grumpy and demanding Kurokawa. The pair travel to Germany on a research trip at the Junkers' factory. They are impressed by the technology the German engineers are using and how advanced their design skills are.

On his return Horikoshi is promoted and tasked with designing a fighter craft for the Japanese navy but it is not a success. Taking a break at a country resort, he meets Naoko, now grown up, who is also staying there. A German guest at the hotel, Hans Castorp, notices how besotted Jirō is. Naoko and Jirō fall in love and become engaged but Naoko, who is suffering from tuberculosis, declares that they will only marry when she has recovered. Jirō returns to work. However, he is wanted by the Special Police and works secretly at his supervisor's house. Naoko goes to a sanatorium to recover but cannot bear to be apart from him and they marry, with Kurokawa and his wife as witnesses. They are very happy together, although Naoko's condition is clearly deteriorating. Jirō's sister, who has fulfilled her ambitions to become a doctor, warns him that tuberculosis is incurable and that Naoko is seriously ill. Jirō starts work on designing a new fighter plane. He finishes the design sitting beside Naoko's futon. When he leaves to test the prototype,

Naoko, realising that she has not long to live, departs for the sanatorium, leaving letters for Jirō and her family.

The film closes with a dream sequence in which Jirō meets with Caproni once more. He laments that his aircraft were used for warfare, noting that not a single plane returned. Caproni reassures him and invites him to his house for a drop of wine.

Art and aeronautical engineering embracing in a romantic drama is an unusual choice of narrative in a career that produced some of the finest fantasy feature films of all time. It's a story set in the real world and one that is extremely moving. Even Miyazaki had to admit that, on first viewing, he had been moved to tears, the first time he had ever cried at one of his own films! Miyazaki had originally planned to make *Ponyo 2* but Suzuki Toshio was not keen on this concept: 'I have absolutely no interest in sequels. I am interested in new themes. If not I have no motivation. I thought this was going to be Miyazaki Hayao's last film so I proposed that he make *The Wind Rises*' (*Sight and Sound* interview, June 2014). As enjoyable as *Ponyo* was, this is perhaps an understandable decision and one that is distinctly Ghibli. 'Our attention will be directed towards the portrayal of people. I want to create something that is realistic, fantastic, at times caricatured, but as a whole, a beautiful film.' Miyazaki adapted the animation of *The Wind Rises* from his own manga that had appeared in *Model Graphix* magazine. He had created a number of works for this publication previously, including the world's most renowned porcine pilot, who became *Porco Rosso*.

The Wind Rises is ostensibly a biopic and its central character was very real, although the protagonist's story has been heavily reinterpreted. Horikoshi was a designer of Japanese aircraft for Mitsubishi, creating, among others, the A6M3 Zero, a long-range fighter plane known for its speed and manoeuvrability, as well as its use on kamikaze missions in the latter stages of World War

Two. Miyazaki himself had a connection with the Zeros as his father's company manufactured parts for these planes. There are many influences for these fictionalised elements of the story, for example Naoko's character and the tuberculosis theme can be found in *The Wind Has Risen* (*Kaze Tachinu*, 1937), a novel written by Hori Tatsuo that depicts a female character struggling with terminal tuberculosis in a Japanese sanatorium. (The real Horikoshi did marry, but his wife did not suffer from tuberculosis.) The German gentleman Horikoshi meets at the resort is called Hans Castorp, the name derived from the novel *The Magic Mountain* (*Der Zauberberg*) by Thomas Mann. In Mann's book Castorp is the main protagonist who visits a cousin (who is also suffering from tuberculosis) in a mountain sanatorium. However, Castorp himself becomes ill and has to remain in this insular little world for many years. In *The Wind Rises*, Castorp is a wise but slightly mysterious figure who, when he strikes up a conversation with Horikoshi, correctly surmises that he has visited Germany and then goes on to anticipate future events in Asia, including Japan's invasion of China and World War Two.

Other real aircraft designers also appear in *The Wind Rises*, although once again their roles in the story are generally fictionalised. Giovanni Battista Caproni appears throughout the narrative, in Horikoshi's dreams, and serves as his inspiration. Caproni was an aeronautical engineer who founded the Caproni aircraft manufacturing company which started building aeroplanes just a few years after the Wright Brothers' historic flight. Caproni was a pioneer who saw the potential for aircraft to be used as a means of passenger transportation. He also built planes designed for war, including bombers, transport and reconnaissance planes; indeed, the Caproni Ca.309 Ghibli was used in World War Two and would also become renowned as the name of Japan's premier animation studio. In the film, Horikoshi visits the Junkers manufacturing plant in Dessau, Germany to learn about aircraft technology, noting how far advanced the German designs are over their Japanese counterparts. As is alluded to in the film, Hugo Junkers was known for creating aircraft entirely from metal and for designing passenger planes. A committed pacifist, he was uncomfortable about aeroplanes being used for the purposes of war but was forced to develop and produce aircraft during World War One by the German government. In the mid-1930s, the Nazis appropriated his patents and had him arrested. He died before the military aircraft bearing his name were developed and used by the Luftwaffe. And Honjō Kirō, the engineer depicted as Horikoshi's friend and colleague, worked for Mitsubishi and designed bombers that were used during the war.

Miyazaki 'scripted' the story by developing a set of illustrated storyboards. When Suzuki Toshio read them, his first comment was that he felt the film was strongly anti-war. Miyazaki felt that Horikoshi wasn't militant at all and wanted to portray that sentiment throughout the film. Any references to (from Horikoshi's perspective) future world events are made indirectly, from Castorp's predictions of war to the pilots who fly past in Horikoshi's dream at the end of the film, a neat device that Miyazaki uses to acknowledge history, but without these greater events overshadowing the intimacy of his story, which is primarily about love and engineering. Jirō is the central creator but this is, despite the historical and political ramifications, as an instigator of work that is astonishing and beautiful, even if its end use is for dreadful purpose. He draws, constructs and oversees the aeroplanes' manufacture as an enthusiastic young engineer. Indeed, at one particular design meeting, Horikoshi notes that the aircraft's weight will be acceptable if they omit the guns. As Miyazaki stated in the documentary *The Kingdom of Dreams and Madness*, 'You know people who design airplanes and machines, no matter how much they believe what they do is good, the winds of time eventually turn them into tools of industrial civilisation. They're cursed dreams. Animation too.'

A rather unusual choice was made for the voice of Horikoshi. Miyazaki and Suzuki had struggled to find actors who had the characteristics needed to reflect the language of the time – 'intellectuals had good diction and higher voices' – and settled on a surprise choice in the form of Anno Hideaki, who had launched his career animating the Warrior God on *Nausicaä* and, of course, was the talent behind the remarkable and hugely influential *Neon Genesis Evangelion* (1995). On realising that it was a personal request from Miyazaki, Anno agreed to an audition and got the job. 'How could I say no to Miya-san?'

In Japan the new Miyazaki film achieved the box-office supremacy expected of it, but despite the stellar results (it was the highest-grossing box-office hit of 2013) there were some controversies surrounding the release. It was criticised in some quarters for glorifying a man who designed machines that were used for warfare. On the one hand the inspirational story, characterisation, animation and emotion were clearly appreciated by audiences and critics alike; on the other, elements of the story, perhaps most notably the nature of a drama that was set in the real world, felt like an anticlimax for those who had been enchanted by the fantastical, magical elements of Miyazaki's previous films. *The Wind Rises* was nominated for the Best Animated Feature Oscar but lost out to Disney's *Frozen* (2013). However, in November 2014 Miyazaki was introduced by Ghibli aficionado John Lasseter to receive an Academy Honorary Award. He noted that times were changing. 'I think I've been lucky because I have been able to participate in the last time that we can make films with paper, pencil and film,' he stated. In Japan he announced his farewell at a press conference in

September 2013. 'I've mentioned that I would retire many times in the past, so a lot of you must be thinking "Oh, not again". But this time I am quite serious.' But, of course, his retirement wasn't to last long. He eventually started working on another animation, which became *The Boy and the Heron*.

The Tale of Princess Kaguya
(Kaguya-hime no monogatari) (2013)

Directed by: Takahata Isao
Written by: Takahata Isao and Sakaguchi Riko

'Even a princess can sweat and laugh out loud sometimes.'

Sanuki no Miyatsuko is a poor bamboo cutter who lives with his wife in the forest. One day he spies something sprouting beside a glowing bamboo cane. It's a small child! He takes this new-found baby girl home and he and his delighted wife decide to raise her as their own, treating her as a divine gift. She grows very quickly, maturing from a baby to a child. The local children call her Takenoko – L'il Bamboo – but this doesn't bother her and she befriends them all, especially the eldest of the bunch, Sutemaru. Sanuki discovers that the bamboos are yielding golden nuggets and the finest kimono. He decides to reject his humble mountain life and go to the capital city where his daughter will fulfil her obvious destiny to become a princess. Having built a grand palace he entreats her to leave the countryside and hires Lady Sagami to educate the girl in etiquette, grooming and musical prowess. When she comes of age she is given a name – Princess Kaguya, which means 'shining light'. However, she yearns for her life in the countryside and, when she overhears the local gentry mocking her father for using attained wealth to obtain a position in the echelons of elite society, she runs away, returning to the forest to find her friends, but they have moved away. She falls unconscious and is returned to the festivities as though she had never departed.

Her growing beauty – often talked of but seldom seen – has turned her into a figure of desire as countless suitors seek her hand in marriage. Princess Kaguya does not wish to marry anyone, so she commands the prospective husbands each to fulfil a task in order to claim her hand. These tasks are unorthodox, fantastical, and impossible to achieve. In turn, the suitors use their wealth or some means of deception to succeed, but all of them fail. Princess Kaguya is astute and the aristocrats are revealed to be charlatans, or they die in their attempts. Even the emperor, enamoured by her beauty, desires her but his lust revolts the girl so she calls on her magical talents and disappears. Literally. As she glances towards the moon she confides her anxieties to the sky. And it is people from the moon who hear her desires, for that was her home world, and she will return there at the next full moon, the memories of her experiences, friends and troubles discarded as though they never existed

The Tale of Princess Kaguya is based upon a well-known Japanese folk story – *The Tale of the Bamboo Cutter* – which is over a thousand years old. The story has been filmed a number of times before, notably as Ichikawa Kon's *Princess from the Moon* (*Taketori monogatari*, 1987), a live-action recreation where traditional culture meets science fiction. Takahata's animation adds a fantastical spiritual element to the fairy tale which enhances the original story. The creation of *The Tale of Princess Kaguya* was long, innovative and fascinating; as Takahata himself noted in *Empire* (April 2015), 'I didn't intend to make the film myself, but I thought it would be interesting.' In many ways this is an animation that takes an ancient tale and films it in a way that reflects the artistry of the time of its creation but develops it in a manner that is distinctly contemporary. Indeed, during the filmmaking process Takahata took the animators outside the normal Ghibli premises to focus on production. The initial plan for release was as a double bill with *The Wind Rises* but that was not to be. As the documentary *The Kingdom of Dreams and Madness* notes, Takahata 'has never delivered on time or on budget' and therefore the release was held back until the film was finally completed. It might have been difficult to convince distributors to take on the real and fantasy double bill (as with the early double bill of *My Neighbour Totoro* and *Grave of the Fireflies*) as both films are significantly over two hours long, unusual for animated films.

Part of the reason for the unusual length of the film is that Takahata embellishes the fairy tale. The original story is very much plot-driven – the discovery of the princess, the suitors' quests for her hand and her return to the moon, but Takahata added a number of elements, most notably Sutemaru's character, and chose to focus on the characterisation. Kaguya is presented as a child of nature. She clearly loves her adoptive father and wants to please him, but he wrongly assumes that the gold that has literally been showered upon the family should be used to elevate her to a high social status. As she comments, 'The happiness you wished for me was hard to bear.' She is required to pluck her eyebrows and blacken her teeth, reflective of the accoutrements of a lady at that time, but this is something that is anathema to her. She yearns to return to the forest where she grew up. Her mother helps her to cultivate a garden, a miniature replica of their homeland and a place where Kaguya finds sanctuary from the formality and rigour of the life of a princess. Her true desire lies with Sutemaru, the peasant and occasional thief who still adores her years later (even after his marriage to another woman and the birth of their child), as Kaguya learns when she visits him prior to her return to the moon. Elements of Kaguya's rejection of rich society can be seen in Takahata's previous work, particularly *Heidi, Girl of the Alps* in which Heidi similarly seeks to leave a well-to-do family and return to the mountains – the place where she can truly be herself. There is a sequence very similar to a scene in *Heidi* where Kaguya discards her formal clothing, running free, fulfilling her desire to return to the natural world. Takahata references many other themes that appear in Japanese culture, including letters or poems being sent from the suitors to the princess with a sprig of flowers or blossom from a specific tree attached, as recounted in the *Tale of Genji* (*Genji Monogatari*), written by the lady Murasaki Shikibu in the eleventh century, which described in very great detail the court etiquette of the time. The ending, depicting Kaguya's family descending to Earth is filled with Buddhist imagery – the Amida Butsu comes to collect her – and reminiscent of the treasure boat in *Pom Poko*, which transports the deceased *tanuki* to heaven.

Takahata's project has resulted in a highly unusual form of anime, most notably with its visual design, which has such a distinctive style. Rather as in *My Neighbours the Yamadas*, Takahata pushed the boundaries of what was perceived to be normal in anime from a design perspective, resulting in a finished production that is as artistic as can be imagined in anime or any form, a combination of inked pen and watercolour or pastel art. The artwork often references the compositions seen in traditional woodcuts or scrolls. Takahata also shuns the use of consistent background art, occasionally showing the characters set against a blank canvas. Particularly interesting is the boldness with which he sometimes literally sketches out scenes – characters occasionally lose form and shape before the art reacquires definition and detail. The scene where Kaguya returns to her hometown during her naming banquet is almost abstract in execution, as she runs away leaving trails of colourful kimono in her wake. It's remarkable because the animation feels so organic and fluid yet is meticulously conceived and animated with absolute precision. The imaginative soundtrack was composed by Joe Hisaishi, who is, of course, most famous for his collaborations with Miyazaki. Often using traditional instruments, the music reflects the tunes and rhythms of the time, especially when Kaguya becomes proficient in playing the *koto*.

The Tale of Princess Kaguya was well received critically and was nominated for an Oscar in the Best Animation category in 2015. It lost to *Big Hero 6*.

When Marnie Was There (Omoide no Mānii) (2014)

Co-written and directed by: Yonebayashi Hiromasa

'I wish for a normal life every day.'

When Anna suffers an asthma attack, her foster parents send her to a quiet seaside town near Kushiro, where she can recover. She is to stay with Setsu and Kiyomasa, her foster mother Kiyoko's relatives. They are a laid-back couple and let Anna roam freely around the local area. She is particularly fascinated by a grand old house near the tidal marshes and goes to visit it at low tide, stepping carefully through the swampy ground. It appears abandoned and dilapidated. Anna falls asleep and is trapped by the tide, and is rescued by local fisherman Toichi. On glancing back at the derelict building, she thinks she notices that the house is lit up.

Anna tries to fit in with the new community but has always found it difficult to make friends. On the evening of the Tanabata festival, she insults one of the local girls and runs back to the marshes. There, she spies a boat and rows – badly – to the old house, whereupon she meets Marnie, a vivacious girl with long blonde hair. They become friends, spending time together. One evening Anna joins Marnie and her parents at a party, dressing up as a flower girl. She watches Marnie dance with her friend Kazuhiko and later Anna and Marnie dance together. But the following day Anna returns to the mansion, only to find it unoccupied once more. She draws pictures of her friend in her sketchbook and meets a local artist, Hisako, who also nurses a fascination for the building. Hisako comments that Anna's drawings remind her of a girl who used to live at the mansion many years ago. Apparently the house is currently being renovated and a new family will move in soon. On her next visit to the mansion Anna meets a young girl called Sayaka, who initially believes Anna's name to be 'Marnie' because she has found a diary hidden in the old house.

Marnie reappears the following day. The girls tell each other about their unhappy family lives. Marnie is bullied by the nanny and servants. The maids once tried to frighten her by taking her to the silo on the hill. The girls go to the silo in stormy weather to cure Marnie's fear, but Marnie abandons Anna, who runs from the building scared and distressed. Sayaka and her brother find Anna and she is taken home with a severe fever. Anna dreams of Marnie and goes to the house once more, where Marnie begs Anna's forgiveness. Later Anna and Sayaka meet Hisako, who recounts the tragic story of Marnie's life. Kiyoko travels to Kushiro to collect Anna and gives her a picture of the mansion, telling her it belonged to her grandmother.

Yonebayashi Hiromasa followed his feature-film debut, an anime based on a 1950s British children's book, with an anime based on a 1960s British children's book. Joan G Robinson wrote *When Marnie Was There* in 1967. Originally titled *Marnie*, its name was changed because Alfred Hitchcock's psychological thriller of the same name had been released some years before. Set in Norfolk, England, the book has a very strong sense of place and, according to her daughter, the character of Anna was influenced by Robinson's own childhood feelings, especially her need to appear to try to fit in and be 'ordinary'. The anime adaptation (co-written by Yonebayashi with Niwa Keiko and Andō Masashi) is generally faithful to its source, but compresses the ending and omits some of the characters from Sayaka's large family. As with *Arrietty*, Yonebayashi made the decision to transplant the action to Japan, setting this tale on Japan's northernmost island of Hokkaidō, with Anna moving from that island's capital city Sapporo to the coastal area near Kushiro. Crucially, the anime has retained the maritime location, notably the tidal marshes as well as the birds that populate them, which feature so prominently in the book. Although lead protagonists Anna and Marnie retain their original forenames, other characters are given Japanese names, the taciturn local fisherman Wuntermenny (so named because he was the last child in a family of 11) becoming Toichi and Scilla becoming Sayaka, for example.

In many ways a young protagonist discovering mystical environments without the support of parental figures is inherent in much of Ghibli's fantasy output and here this premise is given a spiritual dimension where troubles from the past manifest themselves in a society of the present, with often difficult consequences. Anna is a melancholy girl, like Chihiro from *Spirited Away*, although in this instance her misery derives from the fact that she is an orphan, troubled by the fact that her foster mother is being paid to look after her. No one is actively unkind to her, but she just feels different and awkward and finds it difficult to engage with anyone. And she hates herself for feeling that way. That she can befriend Marnie is a step towards allowing herself to be happy.

The narrative is designed to tread a fine line between fantasy and reality. The world Anna inhabits is very real and remains so, but throughout the film we are given indications that Marnie may or may not be real, even though, as an audience, we want her to be real because we witness the positive impact she has on Anna. The mansion's appearance is different every time Anna looks at it; she can never tell whether it will be derelict or beautifully decorated with light streaming from the windows and the sound of music and chatter filling the air. The uncle mentions that the abandoned house may be haunted, populated by ghosts – which reinforces the perception that Marnie may be an apparition. Additionally, Marnie often appears in Anna's dreams. Even Anna convinces herself that her friend must be imaginary, just someone she made up. When they first meet, Anna notes, 'You look like a girl from my dreams.' But, despite this friendship that may or may not be real, it is real enough as far as Anna is concerned and it marks a spiritual journey. More importantly, she develops a sense of self-esteem, and this gives her the opportunity to form real friendships. The revelation that Marnie was Anna's grandmother gives Anna a sense of identity that she has never previously had, having been adopted at the age of two. Kiyoko admits that she is indeed paid an allowance to look after Anna but, although the money helps, she adopted the girl because she *wanted* her and loves her. When Anna finds her family – her real one and her adoptive one – she can finally bring herself to call Kiyoko 'mother' rather than 'auntie'. The Japanese title of the film literally translates as 'Marnie of Memories', a fitting name that sees Anna – through her friendship with Marnie – coming to terms with the changes in her life, accepting her past and learning to be part of a community.

As with *Arrietty*, Yonebayashi's animation is solid but occasionally lacks finesse. Some sequences stand out, however, most notably the silo scene where the intensity of the storm marks the film's most gothic moment, reminiscent of old Hammer or Universal films. Because there is a significant amount of plot to get through, especially concerning the revelations as to who Marnie is and her relationship with Anna, the ending feels slightly rushed. The theme song was written by American singer/songwriter Priscilla Ahn who, inspired by the story of Marnie, identified very strongly with Anna's character and sent her song 'Fine on the Outside' to Studio Ghibli. It was picked up by producer Nishimura Yoshiaki, who liked it so much that he decided to use it in the film.

When Marnie Was There is an engaging and occasionally moving coming-of-age drama which embraces personal relationships and adventures as well as spiritual elements of another time. It did well at the box office but did not top the Japanese charts. Following the release of the film and the announcement concerning the halting of production at Studio Ghibli in 2014, Ghibli producer Nishimura formed animation company Studio Ponoc. Its first feature film *Mary and the Witch's Flower* (*Meari to Majo no Hana*, 2017) was directed by Yonebayashi. This is a delightful fantasy film that is highly reminiscent of Ghibli's output in style and theme and, rather like his first two features, is also based upon a children's book by a British author: *The Little Broomstick* by Mary Stewart.

Earwig and the Witch (Âya to majo) (2020)

Directed by: Miyazaki Gorō

A baby is left on the doorstep of St Morwald's Home for Children orphanage by her mother who has fled from the coven of the 12 witches. The only clue as to the child's identity is a music cassette tape and a note naming her as Earwig (Āya). The Matron names her Erica Wigg, despite the clear indication otherwise. Earwig loves growing up in this environment. Her best friend is a boy named Custard, with whom she shares a love of reading. A born leader, she ensures that she can get everyone to do just what she wants. The orphanage aims to find permanent homes for the children but Earwig is quite happy there and does her best to deter potential families from choosing her. So it comes as a surprise when, despite her protests, a strange-looking couple, short, stout Bera Yāga and tall, thin Mandorēku, decide to adopt her.

Sadly, the reality of her new home does not match expectations and she is virtually incarcerated, forced into doing menial, often very smelly, tasks to arrange ingredients for Bera Yāga, who is a witch. Earwig hopes that her education may at least involve learning some magic but Bera Yāga simply wants a lackey to help further her spell-casting businesses and to make sure that she doesn't disturb Mandorēku. Fortunately Earwig befriends a similarly disgruntled companion in the shape of black cat Tōmasu, a familiar who can help explain the magical processes. Together they come up with a detailed plan to concoct an intricate spell to protect themselves from Bera Yāga's nefarious threats.

The house is full of secrets – hidden entrances, disappearing doors and unorthodox means of getting from one room to another. Moving around is often restricted by Mandorēku's demons and sometimes depends on time and circumstance. Earwig is curious to learn about the cassette tape in her possession and manages to find batteries to play the music on an old tape recorder. Whilst trying to find a means of escape from the house she discovers an ancient and rusty yellow

Citroen 2CV in a hidden garage. Inside is a vinyl record – *Don't Disturb Me* – by the band Earwig. Curiously the song is identical to the music that is on her cassette.

When Earwig magically creates a literal extra pair of hands, welded to Bera Yāga's body, the witch carries out her threat of raining worms upon the young girl. But Earwig's spell protects her and she sends the worms – inadvertently, she thinks it's the bathroom – into Mandorēku's room. He is furious but they reconcile. Through her new powers Earwig begins to make her mark upon the household and life becomes much easier. Even better, she gets to see Custard and at Christmas a very, very special visitor arrives at the house.

Like *Howl's Moving Castle*, *Earwig and the Witch* was based upon a book by Diana Wynne Jones although this time the fantasy and magic are set in the real world rather than an alternate universe. Bera Yāga earns money by selling spells that are mundane but unethical, such as preventing a customer's rival getting a leading role at a dance performance or ensuring that a client's pooch wins first prize at a dog show. This links with *Kiki's Delivery Service*, although Kiki's mother's workshop is considerably more organised than Bera Yāga's and her spells are more beneficial and benign. The film's narrative closely follows that of Wynne Jones's book, which is aimed at younger children, but here it embellishes Earwig's back story.

Amidst the magic, the incarceration and the family history, *Earwig and the Witch* takes standard children's genre tropes – that of a protagonist denied parental influence facing troublesome situations generated by wicked rivals – but embraces and celebrates these traits. Earwig herself has an incredibly forceful personality and absolute confidence in everything she does. In an interview on Anime News Network in June 2020, Suzuki Toshio noted that 'if Pippi Longstocking (the children's literary character whom Miyazaki Hayao had long wanted to animate) is the strongest girl in the world, then Earwig is the cleverest girl in the world'. He described Earwig as 'cheeky, yet somehow cute'. Earwig is very reminiscent of Chie the Brat from *Downtown Story* – self-assured and very independent.

Music is central to the film and its various styles underpin Earwig's situation, her environment and, especially, her past. Inside the house music fulfils a number of functions, first in Mandorēku's prog rock noodlings and compositions that occasionally blare into her confined bedroom but also through the music on the cassette given to her by her mother. This tape represents her past and, perhaps her future, which is emphasised when she chances upon pictures of the band and their album in Mandorēku's room. However we, the audience, always have far more information about Earwig's backstory than she does.

Earwig and the Witch is only the second Ghibli film to be made as a TV movie, for Japan's national broadcaster NHK, who are also credited as co-producers. It was originally scheduled to premiere at the Cannes Film Festival in 2020, but unfortunately the event was cancelled due to the Covid pandemic. It premiered at Lyon's Lumière Festival on 18 October 2020. The film's TV premiere took place on 30 December 2020 and was broadcast on NHK, timely for Japan's new year holiday.

Importantly, *Earwig and the Witch* also marks the studio's first film to made be entirely in 3-D CG. Ghibli had used a degree of CG on previous films, and indeed *My Neighbours the Yamadas* was fully rendered using computers, but it had never created a fully 3-D CG production. Miyazaki Gorō's half-cel, half-CG television anime *Ronja, the Robber's Daughter* proved a welcome introduction to the CG world that has dominated production of animated feature films in recent years. Visually *Earwig and the Witch* – at times – seems to have a stop motion feel to it, with the smooth characterisation and physical movement rather than the texturisation and overtly photo-enhanced detail in rendering. It attempts to achieve a balance between the style of stop-frame 3-D environments with the colourisation of cel-based animation. The result is visually engaging but lacks the organic feel of other Ghibli films. Miyazaki Gorō noted, 'I was the only one among the people at Ghibli who knows that method of creation, so I was able to push the project forward without consulting with anyone. Hayao Miyazaki told me to go ahead with it, and producer Toshio Suzuki encouraged me, saying that it seemed like a fine idea, but after that, I was left to my own devices. I was basically abandoned, so I made the anime with a young staff and didn't consult with the old guys at all.'

While this is most definitely Miyazaki Gorō's vision, there are plenty of references to Miyazaki Hayao's works and they are occasionally very funny. The opening of a mad car chase with a monumentally fast Citroen 2CV recalls *The Castle of Cagliostro*, the filthy chores of an incarcerated child echo *Spirited Away*, and, amusingly, a final credits sketch has Earwig watching *Howl's Moving Castle*.

If there is a criticism it is that the ending of the film seems a touch abrupt, it feels almost as though this is a pilot for a series of wider adventures. Perhaps it is saying that Earwig herself has come of age and will seek to develop her skills, encouraged by her mother's reappearance in her life, but for the audience this is inconclusive. To be fair, the book ends similarly abruptly. In an interview Suzuki hinted that Miyazaki Gorō could make two films, but Studio Ghibli has never made a full sequel and, at the time of writing, nothing has been announced.

The Boy and the Heron (Kimitachi wa Dō Ikiru ka aka How Do You Live?) (2023)

Written and directed by: Miyazaki Hayao

Miyazaki Hayao's declarations of retirement from making feature films, as we have seen, became something of an expected statement following the release of pretty much every film he has made over the last 25 years. And so it was again after *The Wind Rises*. Indeed, this announcement was thought to have heralded the beginning of the end for Studio Ghibli. But in 2016 it was revealed that work had begun on Miyazaki's 'surprise' return to feature film making. The film's title was to be *How Do You Live?* and its release was initially mooted to coincide with the 2020 Tokyo Olympics. Pandemic aside (which also delayed the games) in retrospect it seems that such a possibility was unrealistic, given that in December 2020 Suzuki Toshio stated, 'The film is now half-finished... it will likely need another three years to finish the second half.' Only Studio Ghibli could have the luxury of making a film with no deadline. And, after several years of waiting, a release date of 14 July 2023 (in Japan) was announced.

The studio's marketing of the film was boldness itself: no previews, teasers or trailers. And the Ghibli brand was so strong that no revelations were necessary, only a single distinctive poster of a birdlike character. When the film opened it was a smash at the box office, grossing $13.2 million (1.83 billion yen) in its opening weekend. Just two months later it had already reached the top 20 grossing animations of all time in Japan. The rest of the world had to wait with eager anticipation. For international audiences, the title was changed to *The Boy and the Heron* rather than a direct translation of the original Japanese title.

Three years after the start of World War Two, sirens' shrill sounds warn of an air raid as bombs rain down upon the city, engulfing it in flames, the embers dancing danger in the skies. Twelve-year-old Mahito realises that the hospital, where his mother is receiving treatment, is on fire. Sadly, she is killed in the flames. Years later Mahito is evacuated to the countryside, where his father Maki Shoichi owns an aircraft munitions factory, and is introduced to Natsuko. Natsuko is his mother's younger sister; now married to Shoichi she is pregnant with their child. The family are to live in a grand traditional residence handed down from Mahito's great-granduncle. It even has a plethora of maids who are delighted to see him, and his luggage, as they rifle through his possessions in search of food or cigarettes. More unusually, Mahito is also greeted by a large grey heron.

Mahito enrols at the local school but he stands out as being much wealthier than his classmates. After getting into a fight he hits his head with a rock, self-inflicting a deep wound. Whilst recuperating at home, he chances upon a novel *How Do You Live?* and discovers that it had been intended for him as a gift from his late mother. Natsuko is also confined to her bed due to complications with the pregnancy. Mahito takes the opportunity to explore his surroundings. In the grounds there is an imposing tower, constructed by the great-granduncle, but it is difficult to access. Mahito's issues with the irritating heron become more complex when the bird starts goading him, its long beak and toothy grin declaring that his mother is still alive: 'I will guide you to your mother.'

When Natsuko awakens, wanders into the mysterious building and disappears, Mahito realises he has no option but to try to rescue her. He is joined by maid Kiriko and the heron. 'He says my mother is still alive. I know it's a lie, but I have to go and see.' He discovers that the heron's body is actually inhabited by a small man. The heron, Mahito and Kiriko find themselves drawn into an expansive library which begins to warp and they are dragged through its treacle-like floor into a whole new world. It is a wide and expansive land full of wonders and dangers. Mahito is attacked by a pod of irate pelicans but rescued by warrior sailor, a younger version of Kiriko, who explains to him he is now inside a very different realm. It is a strange world populated by many denizens, including *warawara* – small creatures who will fly away in order to become born into a different sphere of existence – and a group of vicious and dictatorial parakeets whose leader, the Parakeet King, is particularly awesome in his awfulness. On the side of good is Lady Himi, skilled in the application of fire, who can use her power to aid the *warawara* when they are attacked by pelicans.

Mahito finds Natsuko but she refuses to return as he doesn't accept her as his mother. When Himi is kidnapped by the parakeets, Mahito rescues her and meets great-granduncle. He learns about this universe, its dimensions and the role of 13 magical stones that the former architect used to define this world. He was summoned to carry on great-granduncle's legacy. 'My successor must come from my bloodline.' However, Mahito is mature enough to realise that he isn't free from spite and declines the offer. The Parakeet King breaks the stones and the world begins to collapse. Everyone must return to their own worlds but their exit to reality relies on them getting past the malicious parakeets and traversing a long corridor of doors. Mahito rescues Natsuko and invites Himi to join him but she must return to her own world in order to become his mother. She reassures Mahito that she has no fear of fire. Natsuko, Mahito and the heron (as well as Kiriko) pass through the door which leads back to their world. Some years later, the war has ended so Mahito, his father, stepmother and little brother are to return to Tokyo.

Although there are similarities to many of Miyzaki's (and Ghibli's) films, *The Boy and the Heron* bears the most resemblance to *Spirited Away* in structure and tone. A young protagonist is drawn into a strange and mysterious world and has to endure various hardships in order to rescue a family member, in this instance his stepmother. However, whereas it was Chihiro's parents, whom she knew well and loved, who were the driver for her mission, Mahito has to rescue a relative stranger. Indeed, he constantly describes Natsuko as 'someone my father likes' rather than 'mother' and until he acknowledges her as a family member he cannot bring her home. At the same time, although he does not initially realise it, he is forming a relationship with his own mother, albeit her younger self. This helps him come to terms with his grief. This theme also reflects the primary concept in *When Marnie Was There*. In this instance it is a young boy not only coming to terms with loss but also finding his place in the world, albeit initially within a domain that is strange, disorienting and occasionally frightening.

This is a world of dream logic, Miyazaki plays with time, space and his characters in a complex way where everything both makes sense and doesn't. Here we see the younger versions of the feisty old maid Kiriko as a youthful and energetic warrior and sailor; and Himi, whose magical powers give her the ability to manipulate fire, is Hisako who, we learn, disappeared for a year when she was a girl. One could speculate that great-granduncle, an elderly creator who oversees and alters reality in multiple worlds, represents Miyazaki himself. The architect whose experience has influence in a wider context, whilst at the same time looking to heirs as a prospect for securing a safe artistic and imaginative future, even if there are concerns about the practical realisation of these hopes.

While the theme of flying is very much present, there are only passing references to aeroplanes in the context of the war. Mahito's father works for an aeroplane manufacturer (as Miyazaki's own father did) and we see the product of his work, just briefly. In *The Boy and the Heron* flight lies in the realms of creatures with natural wings: the grey heron, the predatory pelicans and the sinister (and yet strangely hilarious) parakeets. Miyazaki uses flexible stylisation, flitting between realistic depictions and anthropomorphism which give the birds human characteristics, further reinforcing the otherworldliness of this strange universe. Most notably anthropomorphic is the titular heron. When we first see him, he is depicted as an accurate representation of the elegant bird, beautifully detailed in its animation. As we soon discover, he is stalking the boy, so we first get an inkling that something is different when we see him talk and reveal a broad, toothy grin. As his intentions become clear, both visually and in his vocal delivery, the beak reveals the synced teeth of a human mouth which becomes more apparently a bulbous nose and indeed a whole head, and he eventually metamorphoses into a human entrapped within the heron's exterior. This marks the heron's unusual link between both worlds in both personas. Likewise, the parakeets are giant, socially organised birds led by the dictatorial Parakeet King, all of which have malicious intentions, complete with kitchen knives, to eat the protagonists should they get the chance. And yet, when they fly into Mahito's world they instantly transform into realistic birds of conventional proportions.

As could be expected from a film that took many years to create the quality of the animation is exemplary with its combination of fantasy and realism. The richness lies in the details, particularly when animating groups of multiple creatures, reflecting the experience of the animator, still working using traditional hand-drawn techniques. The film contains many subsidiary characters which typify much of Miyazaki's previous works. The *warawara* are very reminiscent of *Princess Mononoke's kodama*, although in this instance we are told of their purpose – to fly away and be born as humans, their facial expressions full of hope. They represent the future but – in a time of war in the real world – they are also vulnerable, prey to the pelicans who feast upon them in a frenzy. The opening scene of wartime destruction recalls *The Wind Rises* and *Howl's Moving Castle* but has particularly strong echoes of Takahata's *Grave of the Fireflies* which similarly sees the death of the protagonist's mother.

The Boy and the Heron is ostensibly based upon one of Miyazaki's favourite books, *How Do You Live,* and the film's Japanese title has retained that name, but anyone seeking to read the book should note that Miyazaki had 'only borrowed the title.' As with many Miyazaki adaptations, some of the themes of a novel offer a starting point and then the director lets his imagination take over, taking the story in a completely different direction. It is easy to see why Yoshino Genzaburō's 1937 novel was one of Miyazaki's childhood favourites. It adheres both conceptually and thematically to the ethos of many of Ghibli's works. It is a charming coming-of-age story, where the protagonist Kopperu discovers not only his place in the world and wider society, but also begins to understand the circumstances of other people. His discoveries are complemented by a commentary by his uncle in the form of notes to his nephew, who can interpret the scientific, political, environmental and moral elements from an adult's perspective. The combination of imagination, a child's perception of their surroundings and their interactions with others are central to the book and the wider ideologies of Ghibli's oeuvre. The book has a cameo in the film as a gift to Mahito from his mother, perhaps reflecting her own year-long journey into the other world, by providing sound ethical philosophy for her child.

OTHER PROJECTS

Ghiblies (Giburiizu) **(2000)**

'Yes! We are Ghiblies! Our neighbours are jealous.'

Aired as part of a TV special, *Ghiblies*, a short, 12-minute piece, was made to showcase some of the up-and-coming animators working at the studio. Essentially a meta-work, the film comprises a series of vignettes looking at a number of characters working at an animation studio. This is very much an experimental piece – the animators are clearly having fun – but it also gives the viewer an insight into the animation process. The first character we are introduced to is Oku, a bipedal pig with a mop of brown hair, who talks about the process of character design. He is drawn first with and then without a mouth, and explains how these sorts of design decisions make the character more interesting to the viewer. The story of Nonaka's first love uses even more stylised characterisation as Nonaka's head is reduced to an ellipse with ears, hair and huge square glasses. The fluid animation, delicate, watercolour backgrounds and single striking use of hand-drawn art rendered in 3-D are styles Ghibli would use in many of the adverts they produced. What is interesting about *Ghiblies* is the way that the animators are mixing traditional media with computer imagery. In the Nonaka example this is done to create something that looks hand-made but would be difficult to animate using traditional means. Other parts of the short are more deliberately jarring in their mixing of media – in one sequence a rendered 3-D CGI model of a money-grabbing accountant is revealed to be a wind-up toy in the cel-animated office. Further experimentation comes with the insertion of live-action footage and photographs into the proceedings to link, for example, the mounds of work on Yukari's desk to various mountains in Japan. Things take an even more surreal turn when it turns out that the head of PR might be an industrial spy, imagining himself as a James Bond-style character but apparently possessing the tail of a fish and floating his way around the offices at Ghibli.

Ghiblies is a quirky little short full of humour and ideas that served as a diverting project for the animators prior to full-scale animation on Spirited Away. Indeed the film shows the characters all together in a big meeting for their 'next big project' before revealing the real workers of the studio at a launch party.

Ghiblies Episode 2 (Giburiizu Episode 2) (2002)

A sequel to the original TV short Ghiblies, Ghiblies Episode 2 continues the bizarre lives of the characters at Ghibli, an animation studio uncannily similar to Studio Ghibli. This is obvious from the opening when the profile of Totoro turns into that of hard-working, lovesick Nonaka-san and the legend 'Studio Ghibli Production' is replaced by 'Studio Giburi Production'. The first film introduced us to the various characters at the studio so Episode 2 just launches straight into the fray with a similarly impressive arsenal of animation techniques, although this time around they are used in a less deliberately jarring fashion. Oku, Nonaka and Yukari go out for lunch at a curry rice shop notorious for its extra-spicy menu and bizarre eating rules that relate to the cost of the meal. Yukari, patronised by the proprietor, takes the level ten curry, which, if she eats it in the allocated time, will result in a 1,000 Yen reward. Other vignettes include a psychedelic stream-of-consciousness trip to a nightclub and a perfectly designed train ride where an increasingly embarrassed Nonaka has to deal with a beautiful girl who has fallen asleep on his shoulder. There's a return to Nonaka's first love in nostalgically drawn pastel shades that recalls both Ghibli's tea adverts and the short *Koro's Big Stroll*.

Ghiblies 2 is a more focused production than the first but still alternates between slapstick exaggeration and wistful nostalgia. At times sweet, at times uproariously funny, it's a veritable smorgasbord of animated morsels. *Ghiblies 2* was originally shown as an added bonus to *The Cat Returns* in Japanese cinemas and is also on the Japanese DVD release of that film. A message at the end of the film indicates that further episodes were intended but, at the time of writing, none has emerged.

ADDITIONAL PROJECTS

Over the years, Studio Ghibli has been involved in a number of projects outside of feature-film production. Some of these are commercial and others are more personal or experimental. Sadly, a lack of space prevents us from being exhaustive.

As we have seen, *Ocean Waves* marked the studio's first major foray into television but they had previously produced a series of TV spots, *Sky-Coloured Seed (Sora iro no tane)* in 1992, adapted from the storybook by Nakagawa Rieko and Omura Yuriko. A grumpy fox and a little boy exchange a seed and a toy aeroplane. The seed grows into a sizeable house, an ark for an increasing array of friendly animals, much to the fox's chagrin. Delightfully animated in a simple, childlike style, the character design pre-empts the look of Miyazaki's later short *The Whale Hunt* (2001). The same year saw a series of five adverts featuring *nandarou* – bizarre, one-eyed, pigtailed, self-replicating creatures. Although four of these spots were cel animated in a sparse, background-free style, one utilises a number of CGI techniques to composite the message 'We love cinema' with the huge 3-D *nandarou* towering over the city skyline, illuminated by Hollywood-style searchlights. Miyazaki explored new technological possibilities with *On Your Mark* (1995), a science-fiction fantasy mini-masterpiece whose impressive city landscapes would have been prohibitively expensive to achieve without CGI, although the look is still very traditional. It was a pop video for popular duo Chage and Aska which was released alongside *Whisper of the Heart* in cinemas. Two renegade policemen risk everything to save the life of a captured, winged girl, determined to set her free from the neon and concrete of the oppressive city. *On Your Mark* contains more action, humour and pathos in its under-seven-minute running time than most feature films. Spectacular gun battles, chases above the futuristic city, cruel experiments, simple moments of contemplation while eating *ramen*, desperation and elation combine in a non-linear tale that, even without the song lyrics, tells a perfectly formed story. Other music videos include *Doredore no uta* (2005), a delightful and surreal animation, in a fluid line style, which follows a female folk guitarist (Haigou Meiko, the artist of the track) as she wanders around in a land of perpetually smiling anthropomorphic insects, a sort of psychedelic-lite music video that matches the feel-good nature of the song. *Piece* (2009), a promotional music video for Aragaki Yui directed by Momose Yoshiyuki, follows our protagonist's walk through the city and a number of shoe crises.

Advertisements provide another means of income for Studio Ghibli, but they do restrict the number they produce. The adverts often relate to their own products, such as the relaunch of *My*

Neighbour Totoro and *Grave of the Fireflies* (1996) or the use of Totoro to promote the Ghibli Museum in Mitaka (2001). This later advert links into one for the convenience store Lawsons, a retail outlet that sells advance tickets for the museum and often has tie-in products for the studio's films, such as the 2001 *Spirited Away* promotion and its subsequent DVD release. Less immediately obvious is the *O-uchi de Tabeyō* ('Let's eat at home') marketing of a brand of convenience foods, including curry rice roux cubes. The adverts were standalone pieces, miniature vignettes of nostalgic Japanese life realised through highly detailed drawings and slow 3-D tracking effects. These succinct little films allow the Ghibli artists to play with different techniques and styles – such as the Shop-One advert (2000) that looks towards *Ghiblies* with its quirky, bespectacled main character Nonaka – and they offer a greater opportunity for experimentation. Spots for an Asahi bottled tea drink (2001) use hurriedly sketched lines and spot pastel washes to show 'life on the go', contrasting with the deliberate playbook style of the KNB spots (2004) or the more traditional animation of the *Yomiuri Shimbun* corporate ads (2004, 2005). Miyazaki Gorō directed another commercial for *Yomiuri Shimbun* in 2009 inspired by the work of manga artist Sugiura Shigeru. Kondō Katsuya's charming family of pen-and-inked cats frolic on the screen for food manufacturer Nisshin Seifun (2010). What makes all these pieces so interesting is their brevity, the economy of design used to tell a story almost exclusively through images.

Aside from producing their own animation Studio Ghibli also promotes other examples of animation from around the world by releasing DVDs under the Ghibli Cinema Library label. Many of these are translated by Takahata Isao into Japanese. The range includes works by Michel Ocelot (*Kirikou et la sorcière* [1998], *Princes et princesses* [2000], *Azur et Asmar* [2006]), *Les*

Triplettes de Belleville (2003) by Sylvain Chomet, a number of Russian animated films and even a reacquisition of Takahata and Miyazaki's *Panda Kopanda*.

Never resting on their laurels, Ghibli also found new directions and animations to produce; not suited to feature-length productions, they enjoyed limited support runs and DVD releases. *The Night of Taneyamagahara* (2006), the directorial debut of celebrated background artist Oga Kazuo (who had worked on *Totoro, Kiki* and *Pom Poko*), is based upon a story by Miyazawa Kenji. *Iblard Jikan* (2007) is a more experimental work from artist Inoue Naohisa (*Whisper of the Heart*) featuring his surreal landscape paintings brought to life through animation. The effect is at once soothing but strangely eerie. The pace is languid but Inoue's use of colour and movement is quite unlike anything else, mesmerising the viewer with slowly moving clouds and undulating grass, astonishing rain effects and *Laputa*-like floating islands in the sky.

Studio Ghibli produced another straight-to-DVD series featuring a variety of documentaries about various subjects that interest the studio. These range from a film about Miyazaki and Takahata's mentor Ōtsuka Yasuo and a 'thank you' letter to John Lasseter (*Lasseter-san, Arigato*) to travelogues that follow Miyazaki as he looks at the life of Antoine de Saint-Exupéry (author of *The Little Prince*) and Takahata visiting Oscar-winning Canadian animator Frédéric Back. The studio's interest in documentary filmmaking had its roots in *The Story of the Yanagawa Canals*. Other works include a look into the making of the Miyazaki-produced CD by singer Kamijo Tsunehiko and a film about the creation of the Studio Ghibli Museum.

Ghibli has also been the subject of a documentary. Sunada Mami's *The Kingdom of Dreams and Madness* (2013) provides a fascinating insight into the workings of the studio, bringing together the opinions of, particularly, Miyazaki and Suzuki, as they worked on their most recent productions. A four part TV mini-series produced by NHK, *10 Years with Miyazaki* (2019), follows director Arakawa Kaku as he makes a documentary about Miyazaki. It offers a fascinating, intimate, personal and very honest look at the animator's life and creative processes.

The dust bunnies made an unexpected return in a *Star Wars* galaxy far far away with *Zen – Grogu and Dust Bunnies* (2022). Popular Din Grogu from Disney's *The Mandalorian* encounters the dust bunnies who after a series of amusing misunderstandings present him with a pretty flower, for which he politely bows. Director Kondō Katsuya's delightful hand-animated short was not his first encounter with the dust bunnies. As a Studio Ghibli regular employee he had worked on a substantial proportion of their films as a key animator and character designer, as far back as *Laputa: Castle in the Sky*, and including *My Neighbour Totoro*, in which the dust bunnies first make their appearance.

THE STUDIO GHIBLI MUSEUM

Perhaps the largest undertaking by Ghibli, indeed an ongoing concern, is the Studio Ghibli Museum. The brainchild of Miyazaki, the manifesto of this modestly sized building in Mitaka, Tōkyō, reveals the commitment to an altogether different museum experience:

> *'A museum that is interesting and which relaxes the soul. A museum where much can be discovered.'* Miyazaki Hayao

It is a truly magical space, designed by Miyazaki to highlight not just his own work but the wider world of animation too. For Ghibli fans the museum is a must-see; a giant Totoro welcomes you at a ticket office, the robot from *Laputa* slowly becomes engulfed in vegetation on the rooftop garden, and there's even a furry *nekobasu* for children to play on. Everywhere you look there are little details: stained-glass windows, cubbyholes, dust bunnies. It's a wonderful and tactile place that demands exploring; the visitor guide is deliberately vague and encourages interaction and exploration. Additionally the museum houses a bewildering selection of storyboards, animation cels and background paintings from Ghibli films. Entrance to this modestly priced museum comes with a ticket to see a Ghibli film at the specially designed cinema, the 80-seat Saturn Theatre. These are not just any Ghibli films but specially made shorts, directed by Miyazaki and others, that can only be seen at the museum and are unavailable on DVD.

In *Koro's Big Stroll* (*Koro no Daisanpo*, 2002), cheeky puppy Koro finds himself lost in the city after his mistress goes to school and fails to shut the gate properly. He has a series of encounters before finally being reunited with his owner, who, distraught, has been papering the town with hand-made posters to try and find him. This charming and delicate film is a richly observed road movie that takes in the township surrounding the Ghibli studio. Interestingly, the backgrounds are all drawn in coloured pencils, lending the film a more storybook feel. More surreal is *The Whale Hunt* (*Kujira Tori*, 2001) in which a class of children build a play boat and find themselves on the ocean waves out to tail a whale. With the aid of some bait they manage to lure their prey but soon find themselves far from home. Fortunately, the whale helps pull them back to the coastline and they all enjoy a celebratory photograph.

Mei and the Kittenbus (*Mei to Konekobasu*, 2002) is a sequel to *My Neighbour Totoro*. Mei befriends a small kitten *nekobasu* (a *konekobasu*) by sharing a sweet with it. The *konekobasu* is just big enough for her to squeeze inside and, later that night, she sneaks out of bed to ride in it, discovering that the skies are filled with masses of *nekobasu* of various sizes, lengths and numbers of tails, all ferrying totoros to the forest. There she meets again with her Totoro, still clutching his umbrella, who shows her to a huge and ancient *nekobasu* in need of her therapeutic caramel. Obviously it is a joy to return to Ghibli's most delightful film and see its mascot back in animated form. The flying sequences in particular have a wonderful 3-D sense of space about them as the *nekobasu* purposefully scamper to their destinations.

The Day I Harvested a Star (*Hoshi o Katta Hi*, 2006) is another collaboration between Ghibli and Inoue Naohisa, who provided the story. Nona trades some sizeable vegetables for a tiny blue rock, hawked by a pair of strange salespeople who look suspiciously like an anthropomorphic mole and frog. The tiny rock glows at night, hovering in the air. Before long, through careful nurturing, Nona has grown a fully working planet, complete with its own weather system. But with this comes responsibility and before long Nona needs to set the planet free, where it can thrive in its own environment, alongside its peers. This odd and surreal film combines wonder with a knowing sense of the absurd.

Looking for a Home (*Yadosagashi*, 2006) is a modern fairytale. A red-headed girl with an unfeasibly large backpack searches for a home in the countryside. She finds a place to stay and, frightened by a heavy storm, runs inside where bugs scatter to all corners like dust bunnies. The forest appreciates her respectful attitude and the spirits reward her with natural produce. What is so striking about this film is the way that it uses sound in an experimental and unusual fashion. All the sounds of nature, from the huge fish that gobbles up her perfectly pitched apple, to the mighty storm, are produced vocally by Tamori, a famous TV comedian, and renowned singer Yano Akiko. These sounds are also rendered visually as animated *katakana*, similar to the way sound is depicted as onomatopoeia in manga. Yano Akiko also provided sound effects for *Water Spider Monmon* (*Mizugumo Monmon*, 2006). A water skater and a water spider fall in love in the perilous world of the pond, where fish and crustaceans threaten their fleeting relationship. A closely observed and poignant film, the scenes of the water carp fashioning air bubbles are particularly delicate in their execution.

The folk tale *Nezumi no Sumō* provided the inspiration for *A Sumo Wrestler's Tail* (*Chuu Zumō*, 2010). This short was written by Miyazaki but directed by Yamashita Akihiko. It tells the tale of an elderly couple, mountain dwellers, who spy a group of mice one day and follow them. It appears that they are participating in a sumō tournament. Recognising some of the furry creatures as rodents who live in their home, the old couple prepare food as sustenance for their future bouts. Miyazaki designed, scripted and directed *Mr Dough and the Egg Princess* (*Pan Dane to Tamago Hime*, 2010), a slightly more surreal tale. The Egg Princess, a strange little creature who wears a loose red dress and has curious mannerisms similar to Ponyo, is the servant of an evil witch, Baba Yaga, whose character design is reminiscent of Yubāba from *Spirited Away*. Forced to do chores, the little egg girl has a miserable life, but it changes dramatically when a ball of bread dough in the kitchen comes to life. She forms a friendship with her flexible floury friend and they decide to run away into the big wide world, a landscape that is partly inspired by Pieter Bruegel the Elder's painting *The Harvesters*. But can they escape the clutches of such an evil and ruthless witch? In the charming *Treasure Hunting* (*Takara Sagashi*, 2011) a rosy-cheeked boy and a rabbit compete with each other in a series of contests, games such as racing or sumō, the prize a simple stick. But somehow the competition always results in a draw. The latest film to date is *Boro the Caterpillar* (*Kemushi no Boro*, 2018), made by Miyazaki who decided to work on a short film following his retirement in 2013. The lead character is a small, furry caterpillar who has recently hatched and is about to discover the world. It is notable for being Miyazaki's first film to be made using extensive CGI processes.

The Ghibli Museum regularly holds special exhibitions ranging from the works of other animators to subjects that take the whim of the curators. One such exhibition was of Victorian-style designs for flying machines, a subject close to Miyazaki's heart. To accompany the exhibition with its drawings and models Miyazaki created a short film *Imaginary Flying Machines* (2002), introduced by a pilot pig, as well as supervising two 'film box' shorts: the documentary *The Ornithopter Story: Fly to the Sky Hiyodori Tengu!* (2002) and the animated *The Invention of Imaginary Machines of Destruction* (2002). *Imaginary Flying Machines* has now reached a wider audience as part of a deal with JAL, and is shown on flights along with the JAL-sponsored *Porco Rosso*. JAL also reprinted Miyazaki's manga on the history of airline food.

The Studio Ghibli Theme Park opened in Nagakute in Japan's Aichi prefecture in November 2022. Featuring five themed areas based upon Ghibli's films, it is located on the grounds of the Expo 2005 Aichi Commemorative Park, which hosted the World Expo in 2005 and exhibited a replica of the house from *My Neighbour Totoro* at that time. Miyazaki Gorō's expertise in landscaping and design led to him taking on the role of park director. As with the Ghibli museum this isn't a conventional theme park so don't expect thrill rides and rollercoasters. Ghibli's Grand Warehouse, The Hill of Youth and Dondoko Forest are open to visitors with Mononoke Village and Valley of Witches still under construction (at the time of writing) and planned to open in 2024. The exclusive films from the Ghibli Museum can be seen at the cinema in Ghibli's Grand Warehouse.

OTHER GHIBLI COLLABORATIONS

Over the years, Ghibli has collaborated with other companies and artists, ranging from helping out on projects by providing technical support to full-scale co-production.

Ghost in the Shell 2: Innocence (Kōkaku Kidōtai Inosensu) (2004)

Ghost in the Shell 2 was Oshii Mamoru's remarkable but belated sequel to his original 1994 film. It was a co-production between Ghibli and Production IG, with Suzuki Toshio taking on a producer role. Set a heartbeat in the future, the film's protagonist, a brooding half-cyborg called Batō, is the catalyst for a deep philosophical examination of the boundaries between man and machine, an attempt to define the meaning of the soul. Batō is investigating a series of murders executed by androids who seem to have turned on their masters. It's a quite astounding work that oscillates between intricate scenes of exquisitely detailed animation, bursts of action and thoughtful introspection.

Ronja, the Robber's Daughter (Sanzoku no Musume Rōnya) (2014)

A TV series directed by Miyazaki Gorō, *Ronja, the Robber's Daughter*, based on Astrid Lindgren's book, in some ways sees a return to pre-Ghibli works in that it is an episodic TV series adapted from European literature. Miyazaki Hayao had failed to get the rights to animate Astrid Lindgren's Pippi Longstocking books for *World Masterpiece Theater* some 40 years previously. *Ronja, the Robber's Daughter* was a co-production with Polygon Pictures. Ronja is the daughter of bandit king Mattis; she was born when a violent storm broke his castle in two. Ronja grows up and enjoys exploring the forest surrounding her home, even if the nocturnal grey dwarves and evil harpies provide some frightening encounters. Exploring the lower depths of her castle home Ronja discovers the way to Hell's Gap and meets another child, Birk, a red-haired boy who is the son of her father's rival bandit king Borka and who was born the same night as she was. Their friendship and the rivalry between their families provides the basis for the development of the series and the protagonists' adventures therein. The combination of Ghibli characterisation and animation composited with contemporary CGI elements that mirror the style of traditional cel animation makes for a lively and engaging series which serves as a sweet childhood fantasy.

The Red Turtle (2016)

Another co-production was the arthouse film, *The Red Turtle*, directed by Dutch animator Michaël Dudok de Wit. He noted,

> *'Studio Ghibli contacted me... They literally said, "we like your short film* Father and Daughter. *We like the look. If you were thinking of making a feature film we would like to produce a feature film together with... Wild Bunch in Paris." Honestly you don't receive letters like that, nobody does... They are my heroes... It's like a dream come true...'* The Red Turtle Exclusive Interview with Michaël Dudok de Wit

A tempestuous storm hurls a man onto the beaches of a desolate island in the middle of the ocean. Seeking to escape his solitude he constructs a raft from bamboo but his repeated escape attempts are thwarted when his floating contraption is struck from below and ultimately demolished. He discovers that it is a large red turtle who has destroyed his rafts. He swims back to the island. Later, the turtle comes ashore. Frustrated, the man attacks it but later regrets his anger and tries to revive it. The turtle metamorphoses into a woman and, slowly, the two begin a relationship. Later, the woman gives birth to a baby boy. The years pass and the couple grow older, very much in love. Their son grows up and swims away with a group of turtles. When the man dies in old age the woman transforms back and returns to the wide, wide ocean.

Oscar-nominated, *The Red Turtle* represents an anomaly in award recognition as one of the few films that is genuinely international in the era of post-silent cinema (in that it is completely free of dialogue in any language), but also distinctly avant-garde in its implementation and execution. The innovative style can be linked to Ghibli founder Takahata Isao, who not only co-produced with Suzuki Toshio in conjunction with Wild Bunch and Why Not Productions, but also served as an adviser and artistic producer. The thematic elements of Ghibli's features – the fantastical, the natural as well as their link between the environment and the protagonists – are themes that prevail throughout *The Red Turtle*. Its style, however, is very minimalist – at times the colour palette is so delicately tinted as to approach monochrome and prime concept narrative takes it away from a human and creature romance (like in *The Shape of Water* [2017]) and Robinson Crusoe and into the realms of art animation. There are delightful details in the animal interactions that are natural but also fantastical, from the crabs that first greet our shipwrecked protagonist and provide constant asides to his struggle, to the other birds, beasts and aquatic residents that mark his new social companions as he adapts to his predicament. This is an emotional film which covers loss, love, anger and redemption in a beautifully filmed context that, within its modest running time, manages to cover the lives of its characters in a wide-reaching but succinct manner to moving effect.

Ghibli also has a subsidiary company, Studio Kajino, created to develop products distinctly different from the Ghibli brand. *Portable Airport* (2004), *Space Station No 9* (2005) and *A Flying City Plan* (2005) are three animated videos for the electro-dance-pop band Capsule. All three have a retro-future style, with angular pastel designs that recall 1960s animations but enhanced by modern techniques. The catchy music is complemented by the distinctive visuals, with their emphasis on magazine culture, make-up, romance and stylish couture set in a future world of space stations and transparent spacesuits.

A more unusual production from Studio Kajino, *Ritual* (*Shiki-Jitsu*, 2000) is a live-action feature from Anno Hideaki, an animator and director who was the voice of Horikoshi Jirō in *The Wind Rises* but who has long held a connection with Studio Ghibli. In the mid-1980s, when he was his early twenties, he responded to an advert in *Animage* magazine and was employed to work on *Nausicaä*, contributing to the complex sequences at the close of the film. In *Ritual*, an anime director returns to his hometown, an industrial urban landscape criss-crossed with railway tracks. He meets a strangely made-up girl with green, butterfly-shaped glasses and a crimson umbrella, who always states that the next day is her birthday. She has a ritual that she is convinced will bring her luck and make her disappear completely from the world. Soon he becomes obsessed with her and the two spend time making a film together as he is trying to break away from animation. But even as the pair become more intimate it becomes clear that the lines between fantasy and reality are not distinct in her mind. *Ritual* is a striking and unusual drama that questions the relationships between animators and their creations, filmmakers and their films. It is far more than just a self-reflexive work, and Anno fills his screen, often changing ratios to get precisely the right composition, with contrasting views of industrial landscapes and brightly designed interiors. Jump-cuts, animated sequences and cryptic dialogue ('Our idle routine, the days I spend with her, like a lukewarm bath') make this an engaging portrait of fragile minds heading towards a predetermined fate. Bookending the relationship between Anno and Ghibli is the short film *Giant God Warrior Appears in Tokyo* (*Kyoshinhei Tōkyō ni arawaru*, 2012), a live-action monster film that was screened as part of an art exhibition. It was co-written by Anno with monster design by Miyazaki (based upon the God Warrior from *Nausicaä*) and features a highly enjoyable but ultimately nihilistic trashing of Tokyo in the spirit of the *kaiju* movies such as *Gojira*.

In many ways a cross between the traditional Ghibli style and the emerging modernity of CGI is the studio's involvement in the world of video games. *Magic Pengel: The Quest for Colour* (2002) is a role-playing game in the Pokemon mould with thoughtful game play where the user interacts using drawings. *Ni no Kuni: Dominion of the Dark Djinn* (Nintendo DS) / *Wrath of the White Witch* (PS3) has a more profound connection. Created by Level-5, known for their Professor Layton puzzle games, *Ni no Kuni* is a role-playing game. A teenager finding himself having to deal with fantastical elements in a world far from his own is a familiar premise, as are the themes of parental absence or loss. Oliver has an accident in a vehicle and is saved by his mother, who later dies. His grief animates a toy she had given him and it evolves into Drippy, a quirky character who tells him of life, death and other worlds and offers Oliver hope that he can bring his mother back. The character design is distinctively Ghibli and a number of key sequences in the narrative were animated by the studio. Additionally, much of the game's score was written by Joe Hisaishi.

BIBLIOGRAPHY

The Cat Returns Roman Album, Japan: Tokuma Shoten, 2002

Ghibli Museum Mitaka Catalog, Tokuma Memorial Cultural Foundation for Animation, 2004

Howl's Moving Castle, Studio Ghibli Library, 2004

Littleton, C Scott, *Understanding Shinto*, Duncan Baird Publishers, 2002

McCarthy, Helen, *Hayao Miyazaki, Master of Animation*, Berkeley, California: Stone Bridge Press, 1999

Miyazaki, Hayao, *Starting Point* 1979–1996, Viz Media (translation), 2007

Miyazaki, Hayao, *Hayao Miyazaki's Daydream Notes*, Japan, 1997

Miyazaki, Hayao, *Kaze no tani no Naushika* Vols 1 and 2, Japan: Tokuma Shoten, 2003 (First published 1984)

Miyazaki, Hayao, *Shuna no Tabi*, Japan: Tokuma Shoten, 2008 (First published 1983)

Miyazaki, Hayao, *Tenkū no Shiro Rapyuta*, Japan: Tokuma Shoten, 2004 (First published 1986)

Miyazaki, Hayao, *Tonari no Totoro*, Japan: Tokuma Shoten, 2004 (First published 1988)

Nakagawa, Rieko and Omura, Yuriko, *Sora iro no tane*, Tokyo: Fukuinkan Shoten Publishers, 2008 (First published 1964)

Ponyo on the Cliff by the Sea Roman Album, Japan: Tokuma Shoten, 2008

Spirited Away Roman Album, Japan: Tokuma Shoten, 2001

Studio Ghibli Layout Designs: Understanding the Secrets of Takahata/ Miyazaki Animation Catalogue, 2008

INDEX

⬤LDCASTLE BOOKS

POSSIBLY THE UK'S SMALLEST
INDEPENDENT PUBLISHING GROUP

Oldcastle Books is an independent publishing company formed in 1985 dedicated to providing an eclectic range of titles with a nod to the popular culture of the day.

Imprints vary from the award winning crime fiction list, NO EXIT PRESS (now part of Bedford Square Publishers), to lists about the film industry, KAMERA BOOKS & CREATIVE ESSENTIALS. We have dabbled in the classics, with PULP! THE CLASSICS, taken a punt on gambling books with HIGH STAKES, provided in-depth overviews with POCKET ESSENTIALS and covered a wide range in the eponymous OLDCASTLE BOOKS list. Most recently we have welcomed two new sister imprints with THE CRIME & MYSTERY CLUB and VERVE, home to great, original, page-turning fiction.

oldcastlebooks.com

   kamera BOOKS creative ESSENTIALS HIGH STAKES cmɔ

OLDCASTLE BOOKS	KAMERA BOOKS	HIGHSTAKES PUBLISHIN
POCKET ESSENTIALS	CREATIVE ESSENTIALS	THE CRIME & MYSTERY CL
NO EXIT PRESS	PULP! THE CLASSICS	VERVE BOOKS